MYTHS & LEGENDS
OF STAMFORD
IN LINCOLNSHIRE
·
COLLECTED BY
MARTIN SMITH
-

KING
BLADUD
FOUNDER
OF
STAMFORD

HENRY
HANNA
FOUNDER OF
THE MEDIEVAL
UNIVERSITY

FOR MUM AND DAD

THE
MYTHS &
LEGENDS
OF
STAMFORD
IN
Lincoln *Shire*

Written and Illustrated by
MARTIN SMITH

PAUL WATKINS *Stamford* MCMXCI

Published by
PAUL WATKINS
18, Adelaide Street, Stamford, Lincolnshire,
PE9 2EN

ISBN
Hardback: 1 871615 64 X
Paperback: 1 871615 69 0

The hardback is a limited special edition of *one hundred*
copies numbered and signed by the author

Designed and photoset at the **Sign of the Cat** by
Martin Smith for Paul Watkins

Printed and bound by Woolnoughs of Irthlingborough

CONTENTS

PREFACE
& ACKNOWLEDGEMENTS

The fury of the armed factions of the Roses, the superstitious fanaticism of the Puritan, and the bad taste of a succeeding generation have left their marks on Stamford; and after inspecting its relics and reading these records the visitor, while he thinks of the things that have been and are not, will be ready to exclaim-
'The evil that men do lives after them.'
Fourteen Parish Churches; Augustine, the Black, the Grey, and the White Friaries; the Priory of St. Leonard; the nunneries of St. Michael and St. Mary; the Colleges of Brazenose, of the Gilbertines, of the Carmelites, and of the Abbeys of Vaudy, Thorney, and Burgh; the Knights Templars' House of St. Sepulchre and the Chapel of St. Mary Magdalen; the Hospital and Church of St. John and St. Thomas of Canterbury; the Hospitals of St. Leger and St. Giles; the gorgeous Eleanor Cross; the suburb of Bredcroft with its chapel and its Court-house; the Military Walls with eleven towers and nine gates; the Saxon Fortress; the Royal Norman Castle overlooking quaint streets often gay with mounted knights in nodding plumes and shining armour. These had Stamford.
G. H. Burton, Preface to *Rambles Around Stamford*, 1872.

OVER THE years I have found numerous snippets of information relating to the folklore of the town in all kinds of obscure and diverse places. When I realised that these had never been properly collated or discussed I decided to put them all together into one volume. Although each myth and legend is given a thorough interrogation the overall emphasis of the book is sympathetic and enthusiastic. The layout is intended to be fun and deliberately copies the style of eighteenth-century books with illuminated letters, floral decorations and arbitrary italics. The book is typeset in Bodoni, an Italian eighteenth-century typeface; the main headings are in Garamond, a Renaissance type, and the commentary sections are in Times Roman, a modern newspaper typeface.

Above all I would like to thank Shaun Tyas (of Paul Watkins) for all his help and enthusiasm. Special thanks to John Smith, Michael Key, Mark English, Dave Roffe, Philip Riley, and Anne Wilkins. I also thank the staff at Stamford Museum, Stamford Town Hall and Stamford Library for their co-operation. I hope you enjoy the book!

Martin Smith, Stamford, 1991.

INTRODUCTION

...the town walls, the 'Callises', the Gothic gateways, the 'Queen Elizabeth', the 'Queen Anne', the monuments - among them the finest of its date - the strange tales and local legends, all these things enhance the air of ancient peace and prosperity in which the town seems to bask - sometimes almost to sleep.
Rev. W. J. Loftie, *Architectural Review*, 1904.

It requires great judgement to distinguish and part out what is truth, when it is bewrapt and clouded with such a heap of fictions.
Francis Peck, *Annals of Stanford*, 1727.

OST OF Stamford's *myths* and *legends* were not born out of popular tradition but were the result of over-enthusiastic antiquarianism. The town's ancient architecture and medieval importance incited historians to speculate freely about the past, with every successive writer knowing just that little bit more than his predecessor. A whole spurious tradition was fostered which entered into the popular history of the town - from Richard Butcher in the seventeenth century, via the eighteenth-century antiquarianism of Francis Peck and William Stukeley, to the nostalgic Victorians such as George Burton, Mackenzie Walcott and E. Bentley Wood. This book is intended to be an entertaining guide to the folklore of Stamford, and it examines for the first time the sources and historical accuracy of the stories.

8

MYTHS AND LEGENDS

It seems sensible to begin a critical account of Stamford's *myths* and *legends* with a brief discussion of what *myths* and *legends* are, and in what respects they differ from one another. It is difficult to define the two terms exactly, because they are often used without distinction, or in a very elastic fashion, changing their meaning according to context. Even experts, despite their sophisticated definitions, have failed to deal with the subject effectively or consistently. A simple distinction will be made here between *myths* and *legends* for the ease of categorising the examples from Stamford.

'Folklore' is a broader (and therefore safer) word to use, but that term embraces every aspect of local culture, from *myths* and *legends*, and traditions and customs, to dialect and cookery. The subject of this book is a little broader than just *myths* and *legends*, but it is narrower than folklore.

Myths

Myths are symbolic accounts which use a quasi-historical background to help to explain man's place in the world. They originally involved tales of gods and super-human beings, but the word is often used to describe any narrative having a fictional basis.

The explanations used in *myths* are not scientific but lie in our own psychology. Many commentators in the twentieth century, such as Frazer, Freud and Jung, have made heavy weather of the psychological origins of myths, but in many cases the myth is there just to confirm the importance and power of a community and also to relieve it of any responsibility for its decline or defeat. Mythologies contain stories of both creation and destruction. Creation stories usually offer an explanation which gives an exaggerated importance to the locality or people and destruction myths always lay the blame on someone else. The creation of Stamford is credited to an ancient British king who built the first university in the world here, and the embarrassing decline in the town's prosperity in the sixteenth century is blamed on the sack of the town in 1461.

9

Legends

Legends differ from *myths* in that they ultimately have a factual basis. The facts may have been elaborated by succeeding generations, but a *legend* must still contain a kernel of truth if it is not to be classed as a *myth*. Commentators have classified *legends* into different categories, of which the most important for Stamford are:

I   Migratory *legends* and *legends* of wars and warriors. Most of the *legends* in the Norse sagas, for instance, fall into this category. In Stamford the most cited are the Roman occupation, the invasion of the Picts and Scots in the fifth century, the Danish invasion, the Wars of the Roses and the Civil War.

II   *Legends* of famous people. The use of the word *legend* here means the man or woman rather than the story (as in the term 'a living *legend*'). They are often allied to the *legends* of wars and in Stamford we have accounts of Boudicca, Hengist, Cromwell and Charles I. There are also stories of outstanding men and women to whom a reputation for wisdom or wizardry has become attached (Roger Bacon, William Stukeley), and others are men of outstanding notoriety. Dick Turpin, the famous early eighteenth-century highwayman, for instance, is supposed to have stayed at the Bull and Swan Inn in St. Martin's where he stole a silver tankard.

III   Local *traditions*. These are memories of comparatively obscure happenings which show how actual events are reshaped in popular thought. Stamford examples would be the medieval university and the sack of the town in 1461. The fact that the sack of the town also has a mythological function illustrates why *myths* and *legends* have become synonymous terms, often linked together in order to avoid the difficulty of deciding which word to use.

Miracles

Miracles are distinct from *myths* and *legends* in that they are marvellous events occurring within human experience, which because of their extraordinary or supernatural character are considered to indicate the intervention of a deity. Many *miracles* have a factual basis and are associated with famous people - Hereward the Wake and St. Hugh of Lincoln for example - but the supernatural element separates them from *legends.* They usually have a religious function (Goethe described the *miracle* as 'the dearest child of faith'), often to demonstrate a moral point or to show how the power of one particular deity is greater than another: the Christian God triumphing over the Devil or pagan gods for instance. There is a huge corpus of medieval accounts of *miracles* and Stamford is the scene of a number of them. Other supernatural tales about Stamford have been grouped with *miracles* for convenience, although they are not of quite the same character.

Customs

Customs are social practices or conventions, often associated with minor superstition or the cycle of the year, which are observed by the people of a locality. In Stamford there is a reference to the common *custom* of informing bees of death and another to the throwing of loaves of bread into the river to find a drowned body, as the bread would not float downstream of the corpse (*County Folklore*).

In a festival a social *custom* involves the whole community. In addition to those which celebrate the turning points of the year (ancient pagan festivals later given a Christian gloss), which are common throughout England, the most obvious festival unique to Stamford was the November bull-running. Rather more drastic than the bottle-kicking at Hallaton, Leicestershire, or the recently revived Straw Bear festival at Whittlesea, near Peterborough, it performed the same social function in that it was an opportunity for the community to escape from the stifling restraints of civilisation and abandon itself to liberal excess. The Lord of Misrule found in the Stamford bull-running was a common character on these occasions. This type of festival (i.e., a day of socially-accepted

11

excess) is rare now in England. The nearest modern equivalent would be the celebration of the New Year.

New Mythology

The twentieth century has seen a revival of 'enthusiastic antiquarianism', comparable to that practised by Stukeley in the eighteenth century, but with the difference that it is now both popular and widespread. Like all *myths*, the new ones contain strong, specific ideas which are not backed by substantial evidence. They express a desire to relate to a lost age of ancient religion, in a context of profound alienation from the modern world.

The new mythology contains much diversity but an emphasis on the environment and its features is its most common characteristic. Belief in the power of the pyramids, the patterns of leylines, 'energies' at Stonehenge and Avebury, or the Glastonbury (and other) zodiacs, are all focused upon particular localities. As in medieval Catholicism, pilgrimage has become important again. The APPENDIX contains, as a local example of the new mythology, a dicussion of the Stamford Taurus.

Conclusion

There is still an abiding interest in all aspects of folklore, because it gives each locality a uniqueness. Even the most bizarre mythology contains poetry which ensures that the tale captures our attention, though its metaphors are difficult to explain. The strange, dream-like tale of Roger Bacon's talking brazen head is more intriguing than an account of his scientific achievements; and a sense of place, found in local culture, has value in a world with an increasingly international outlook. Dr Bergen Evans states in the introduction to his *Dictionary of Mythology*:

> We will not find scientific or historical truths in the mythology, but we will find poetic truth. And poetic truth may be all the truth that men will ever know.

MYTHS
AND
LEGENDS

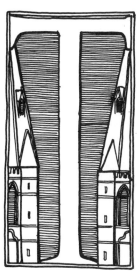

HE *MYTHS* and *legends* of Stamford are collected here in chronological order, beginning with the foundation of the world's first university at Stamford in 863BC and finishing with the foundation of Britain's oldest surviving newspaper, the *Stamford Mercury*, in the late seventeenth century. Each *myth* or *legend* has its own commentary set in a modern newspaper typeface which discusses the origin and validity of the story. All quoted sources are fully documented in the bibliography at the back of the book.

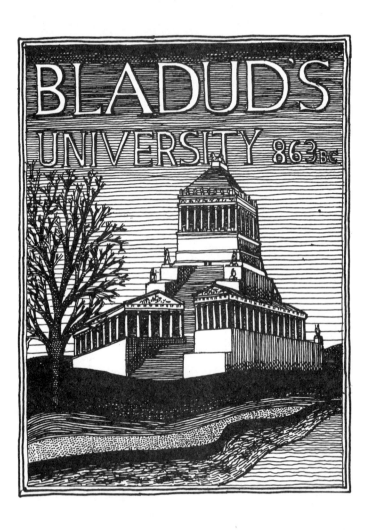

THE
GREAT UNIVERSITY
OF
STAMFORD

For Stamford was erst a university town of renown whose splendid colleges rivalled both those of Oxford and Cambridge and even at one period threatened to supersede them, and probably would have done so but for powerful and interested political intrigues.
James John Hissey, *Over Fen and Wold*, 1898.

The first impression of the Town... reminds the traveller of Oxford. The likeness must have been most striking when the halls of the Monastic Houses of Peterborough, Crowland, Sempringham, and Vaudey, and Brazenose college, were thronged with students, and an academical look was given to the streets by the flowing gowns and various hoods; when the castle keep, the Town gates, and the grey walls; spires, towers, and steeples, and turreted fronts, the quiet quadrangles, the solemn courts and venerable cloisters, the tall roofs, and louvres of numerous churches, hospitals, chapels, convents, and religious houses... rose in the green meadows along the winding banks of the Welland...
Mackenzie Walcott, *Memorials of Stamford*, 1867.

The Ancient University *Myth*

N 863BC, King Bladud, the Trojan king of ancient Albion (or Britain) and the father of King Lear, founded the first university in the world at Stamford. The event was first recorded by the venerable sixth-century wizard, Merlin of Caledonia, the 'British Apollo', and was elaborated by later writers.

After attending the famous schools in Athens, Bladud - who was a descendant of Aeneas of the Trojan Wars - returned to Albion with many wise and learned teachers to establish a place of learning. On the banks of the Welland they found the sylvan setting appropriate for such an illustrious academic institution. The ghost of Bladud tells us:

At last they found a place therefore
Amidst the realm it lies well nighe,
As they by art and skill did proue:
An healthful place not low nor high,
An holesome soyle for their behove.
With water streames, and springs for welles:
And meadowes sweete, and valeyes grene:
And woods, groaves, quarries, al thing else
For studentes weale, or pleasure bene.

When they reported this to me,
They prayde my grace that I would builde,
Them there an Universitie,
The fruites of learning fore to yelde.

I buylte the scholes, like Attike's then,
And gave them landes to maintayne those
Which were accounted learned men,
And could the groundes of artes disclose.

Bladud.

The towne is called Stamford yet...
John Higgins, *The first parte of the Mirour for Magistrates,* 1575

Bladud is usually associated with the building of Bath and its spa baths dedicated to Minerva, but more importantly

To Stamford in this Isle, seemed Athens to transfer;
Wise Bladud, of her Kings, that great philosopher.
Michael Drayton, *Poly-Olbion, Song VIII,* 1622.

Athenian style temples and halls were built by the Welland, probably with long colonnades of beautiful fluted Doric columns carved by Greek masons in the local limestone. These halls

Had Scholars fell of great habilite,
Studieng over all allwey in unite,
In all the seven liberall science,
For to purchase of wisdom and sapience.
John Hardyng, *Chronicle*, completed before 1465.

According to Geoffrey of Monmouth, Bladud died like Icarus, when he fell into the Temple of Apollo at *Trinovantum* (Bladud's pre-Roman London) whilst trying to fly. This event was mirrored in Stamford in 70 B.C. when Simon, an Athenian who established a school in the town, was drowned in the Welland whilst attempting human flight.

The university was later occupied by the Druids, the priest-magicians of the Celtic race. Samuel Sharp in his *History of Stamford* of 1847 says: 'It is most likely... that certain localities... were set apart by the Druids for the assemblage of their pupils and disciples; and why may not Stamford be one of these?' He adds that 'There is little doubt that here existed a town in the time of the Britons' and a settlement grew around the Druidic university which according to Peck was the ancient British city of *Doorebriff*, meaning '*sharp stream*'. Blore, quoting Butcher, states that 'the learning of the Heathens flourished there, until Lucius King of the Britains, about the year 192,... exploded the profession of heathen philosophy' and converted the university to Christianity. Later, in 449 the university and town were attacked by invading Picts and Scots, but Hengist's victory over them, and subsequent decision to build the first Saxon town at Stamford, ensured its future.

A British Druid reproduced from Stukeley's, *Stonehenge*, 1740.

By early Saxon times the university was flourishing:

> And as before it was very famous throughout the world, for the great Proficency of Ethnick learning, so in that time... it much more flourished with Learned, Holy and Religious Men... The fame of whose Piety and learning caused many of the Christian Princes and other Great Men, neighbouring upon the Isles of Britain, to send their Sons and Friends hither, to be taught and educated by these pious Masters.
> **Francis Howgrave,** *Essay on the Ancient and Present State of Stamford,* 1726.

In 601, the monk Austin (Augustine of Canterbury) found mixed Saxon and British students at Stamford University engaged in heretical practice, particularly Pelagianism - a belief which denied original sin and promoted free will. Incensed by this heresy Pope Gregory I suppressed the academy in 605, destroying its ancient halls and former pagan temples until nothing remained of the world's first university.

The Medieval University *Legend*

HE GLORY of Stamford's ancient university was not forgotten. As the town became more prosperous in the twelfth and thirteenth centuries a new and greater university was built on the ruined foundations of the old. Stamford University became England's third medieval academy alongside Oxford and Cambridge and threatened to supersede both. Edmund Spenser in Book IV of his poem the *Faerie Queene*, published in 1596, wrote:

> And shall see Stamford, tho' now homely hid,
> Then shine in learning more than ever did
> Cambridge or Oxford, England's goodly beams.

Which was then adapted by Drayton:

18

Here Stamford (which so much forgotten seems to be)
Renown'd for liberal arts, as highly honour'd there,
As they in Cambridge are, or Oxford ever were:
Poly-Olbion, Song XXIV.

Following the dissolution of a
breakaway university at Northampton
by Edward I in 1264, two hundred
Cambridge and Oxford students,
converted to Pelagianism, moved to
Stamford, where there was already
an established tradition of learning
and heretical practice. Henry
Hanna, the provincial of the
Carmelites, had resurrected the
ancient university when he founded
a school in St. George's Square in
the 1250s. Peck says: 'Henry Hanna

Henricus deHanna Fundator Academiae Stanfordienfis

Henry Hanna from a drawing by
William Stukeley.

was the beginner of Academical education and of the University it self at
Stanford' and that the Carmelites (Whitefriars) were the 'chief
professors and tutors to the youth of this University'. Stukeley in his
diary for 1745, however, claimed that the medieval university evolved
from All Saints' College, established in 1109 at Wothorpe, by Joffied,
Abbot of Crowland Abbey.

After Henry Hanna's hall, the first colleges to be established, as
Peck tells us, were general schools open to all, such as Brazenose
College by St. Paul's Gate. These colleges, though, soon proved
inadequate for the 'all comers who promiscuously flocked from all parts
to this University' (Peck) and other friaries, disliking the mixture of lay
and secular education, established their own schools. Black Hall was
founded by 'some order of Black monks' (Peck) in All Saints' Place,
and the Blackfriars and Greyfriars also had schools in the town. As
these colleges became overcrowded, the large monasteries set up their
own academic halls, including Sempringham Hall and Durham Hall in
St. Peter's Street, Peterborough Hall in All Saints' Street and Vaudey
Hall (owned by Vallis Dei Abbey near Grimsthorpe) in St. Mary's
Street. Each monastic order established a religious foundation in the

19

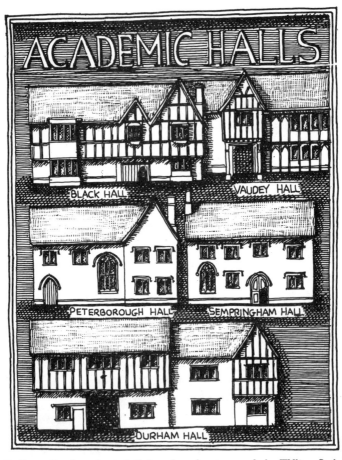

Stamford's medieval academic halls based on drawings made by William Stukeley in *Designs*, 1736.

town resulting in a proliferation of churches until as Samuel Sharp says: 'Stamford... must have been a kind of monastic metropolis.' Butcher comments that 'The Monks, Friers, and Nuns of those superstitious Times (like so many Rats or Mice, which make choice to feed of the daintiest cheese) made choice of this Place to build here several Receptacles...'

A university of such importance was bound to attract the intellectuals of the nation, and Peck lists a whole host of *literati* who worked at the university, including the notable authors William Wheteley, William Ludlington and Walter de Heston.

The most dramatic event in the university's history was the secession in 1333 of northern students from Oxford to Brazenose College in St. Paul's Street. Merlin had miraculously prophesied this event over eight hundred years earlier:

> That studious throng which
> Oxenford doth cherish
> In time to come the Stoneyford
> Shall nourish.
> **John Hardyng,** *Chronicle.*

Here, led by the mysterious H. de R. (A. F. Leach later claimed it was led by William of Barnby, fellow and bursar of Merton College), they established a rebel university away from their argumentative southern counterparts. Apparently Merton College had refused to take northern students and Oxford had been plunged into chaos and riot. A poem written in Stamford in 1334 and addressed to Fitz-Ralph, Chancellor of Oxford says:

> I reject the blood-stained Ford and the horned Ox;
> I change my pasture; I welcome a more fertile spot.
> Beneath the shield of Stamford I prefer to dwell safely.

They even brought with them the distinctive knocker which was later returned to Oxford in the late nineteenth century.

The arrival of the Oxford students, though, was to bring about an untimely end to Stamford's medieval university, for in 1334 Oxford persuaded King Edward III to intervene and close it down:

21

..this new assembly of scholars at the town of Stamford for University instruction [is] in every way hurtful and pestilential.... we beg and beseech you to extirpate by your royal power, so what was begun by improvident rashness may be quickly put an end to by the royal wisdom, and be a warning to future evil-doers.

The sheriff of Lincoln was sent to Stamford, but he met with considerable resistance, and Peck, quoting John Selden, suggests the king himself came to the town because of the students' stubbornness. It wasn't until July 1335 that the academic halls were finally routed and the students and masters expelled.

Thus ended Stamford's prestigious university history, destroyed first by the vengeance of the church and later by the jealousy of Oxford University. Camden states that some of the colleges continued until the Lancastrian sack of the town in 1461, but it was no longer an important university. By the seventeenth century Stamford was just a shadow of its former self. A poem of 1667 from *Drunken Barnaby's Journal* is a sad testimony to a town in decline:

To Stamford came I from where I find
Purses are sold of every kind;
Purses there that cut a flash,
Purses in plenty but no cash;
As many as Vermin as crawl o'er me,
So many beggars are before ye.
Where are the scholars, proctors, fellows, college?
They've into purses crammed their former knowledge.

COMMENTARY
The Ancient University *Myth*

The story of King Bladud was first chronicled by Geoffrey of Monmouth (*c.*1100-1154) in his *Historia Regum Britanniæ*, a collection of mythology and history relating to the early history of Britain, which he claimed he had translated from a lost book of Breton legends. Geoffrey, however, makes no reference to Bladud establishing a university in Britain. John Hardyng, a mid fifteenth-century poet and chronicler, is the first to mention the story and quotes as his source the sixth-century Merlin of Caledonia, more commonly known as Merlin the Wizard. There is no evidence, though, for the existence of 'Merlin' and writings attributed to him are spurious.

This implies that the myth of Bladud's University was invented by Hardyng, and was inspired by the 1333 secession. Blore in 1813 suggested:

> Poetry, like tradition, derives, however, so many charms from fiction, that it is not improbable the lines of Hardinge were rather the authority for *this* than an honest record of *any well-founded* tradition; especially as he is notoriously known to have been an inventor of forgeries.

The tale was then copied by later historians and poets such as John Ross, the late fifteenth-century Warwick antiquary, John Higgins (working *c.*1570-1602), Michael Drayton (1563-1631), and local historians such as Richard Butcher and Francis Peck. John Leland writing in the mid-sixteenth century calls the whole episode a 'dream'. The tale of Simon the Athenian appears in Samuel Sharp's *History of Stamford* of 1847, where he says he found it in a 'quaint old black-letter record'. It is probably a conflation of the Bladud legend with that of Simon Magus who appears in the canonical *Acts of the Apostles* and the apocryphal *Acts of Peter* and who is credited with being the first teacher of the Gnostic heresy. When in Rome

Simon is said to have encountered St. Peter and in an attempt to gain converts he flew through the air supported by invisible demons. St. Peter, seeing this threat, banished the demons and Simon fell to his death. Both Simon and Bladud have fatal attempts at flight, black magic and heresy in common, and it is easy to see that the two stories could have become confused.

The story of the suppression of the university by Pope Gregory I is a fantasy inspired by the historical letters between Augustine and the Pope as recorded in Bede's history of 731. There is no mention of Stamford in these letters and the tale must have been created by Hardyng to fit in with his earlier mythology.

The Medieval University *Legend*

If the story of the ancient university may be classified as myth, the claim for a medieval university may be classified as legend. The word 'university' implies a whole body of teachers and scholars organised under a single corporate administration. The 1333-5 secession from Oxford, firstly to Northampton and then to Stamford, is factual, but the group of teachers and students was never sufficiently large or established to be considered a proper university. Many students returned to Oxford prior to 1335, and only seventeen masters, six parish priests and fourteen students were found in the last inquisition. Had it continued, however, the rebel university could have become a rival establishment to both Oxford and Cambridge. This potential was recognised by both universities. Two years after the secession, Robert of Stratford, the Chancellor of England and Oxford, wrote to Cambridge University with the sobering thought that

> If the said university of Stamford had lasted, it would have been to the disadvantage and dishonour of both universities

and until 1854, Oxford made students swear an oath

...that you will not lecture or attend lectures at Stamford, as in a university or general school or college.

They even took the Brazenose gate knocker to Oxford in 1890 under the impression that it had originally come from Oxford. However, there is no proven evidence that the rebel students ever used the Brazenose site. Brasenose Hall at Oxford was in existence by the mid-thirteenth century and probably derives its name from 'brazen nose'.

Brazenose knocker reproduced from Drakard's *History of Stamford*, 1822.

The earlier secession of Cambridge and Oxford students in 1264 is mentioned only by the historian Richard White (1539-1611) and was copied by Anthony Wood, a late seventeenth-century Oxford writer. It is probably just an elaboration of the historical secession of Cambridge students to Northampton in 1261. The Pelagian connection appears to be just a confusion with the earlier myth.

The arrival of the Oxford students, though, implies that there was an earlier tradition of learning in the town, but this was by no means as significant as some writers have suggested. There is only one adequately documented monastic school, which was founded by the Lincolnshire priory of Sempringham in c.1301. Robert Luterell, younger brother of Sir Geoffrey Luterell, who commissioned the famous *Luterell Psalter*, gave his house called 'the Gannoc' on St. Peter's Street for use as a school, and it had its own chapel of St. Mary. About half a dozen Gilbertine novices lived there, studying theology and philosophy, and the school was possibly attended by other town students (Durham Hall at Oxford, established in 1286, was a similar, though larger, institution, housing sixteen students). The existence of this school suggests that there could have been other halls in the town, but there is no definite evidence. It is known that St. Leonard's Priory had some academic function, for in the fourteenth century it was partly used as a study centre for young monks, possibly preparing them for their degree courses at Oxford. Alan Piper suggests that St. Leonard's was quite a prestigious academic institution, run by masters of 'high calibre in terms of administrative experience and intellectual training'. This teaching function, though, declined sharply after 1380 with the establishment of Durham College at Oxford.

There is no proper medieval evidence for any of the other halls, but they were a common tradition by the sixteenth century. Leland states 'a great voice rennith that sometyme readinges of liberalle sciences were at Staunford', but Brazenose is the only other authenticated medieval building, and it has no academic record. Stukeley's claim for All Saints' College at Wothorpe is based on Speed's early seventeenth-century map, and is just a misreading of an entry in *Valor Ecclesiasticus,* Henry VIII's survey of the value of ecclesiastical property. This merely mentions that Browne's Hospital held property at Wothorpe. Although the Orders of Friars were influential in university life in Oxford there is no proof for their academic activities here. The significance of the Carmelite school has been greatly exaggerated because of the widespread misunderstanding that the Carmelite Whitefriary stood on the site of the hospital, an important monastic site with a splendid fourteenth-century gate. This was actually the Franciscan Greyfriary and the Whitefriary stood just to the south-west between St. Paul's

Whitefriar's gate from a drawing by William Stukeley, 1735.

Street and Priory Road - a much less romantic site. All we know of Henry Hanna comes from Leland, and he never mentions Hanna teaching anywhere or acquiring any eminence, and there is no medieval evidence for his school. William Ludlington in fact taught at Oxford, not Stamford, and William Wheteley was master of Lincoln Grammar School. As for the tradition of monastic halls, Leland implies that the names of many of the buildings (e.g. Peterborough Hall) merely reflected the ownership of the property:

> ...the names of Peterborough Haulle, Semplingham and Vauldier yet remayn there as places for those houses of men of religion that sent their scholars thither to study: except a man wille say that these houses otherwise cumming to them kept theyr names.

Despite this, later writers supposed many buildings to be academic halls. This tradition began with Brian Twyne's visit to Stamford in 1617, was elaborated by Anthony Wood in 1674, and by Peck and Stukeley in the eighteenth century. On Stukeley's arrival at Stamford in 1729 Peck wrote to him calling him 'President of Black Hall, Peterborough Hall, Sempringham Hall, Durham Hall and Vaudey Hall'. Any large medieval building became susceptible to classification, and Peck claimed that inns, such as the Windmill, formerly at no. 51 High Street, were used as halls. Blore says:

> if we are to believe with Peck, that all the houses in the town of Stanford which bear the marks of antiquity, are remnants of Colleges and Halls for education, the whole town must have been full of them.

Even if there were monastic or friary-owned schools in the town they would still not constitute a university, as each school would be administered separately and would be dominated by the beliefs of the monastic order. Samuel Sharp's vision of a 'monastic metropolis' is an exaggerated fantasy and the reason for the large number of churches in the town was not monastic but the result of early self-government and the absence of any single overlord other than the king.

Any academic learning at Stamford, therefore, must have been of limited scope and only the rebel students and masters between 1333 and 1335 ever issued degrees. Small monastic schools, a teaching capacity at St. Leonard's Priory and the temporary residence of the Oxford students cannot constitute a university under a corporate body. Deed in his *History of Stamford School* says that 'although there were halls and places of learning in Stamford there is no evidence that there was any university organisation'. Stamford's main role was probably as a 'cramming' centre preparing novices for Oxford. It was the potential, though, of the 1333 secession that captured the imagination of historians. It spawned the Bladud tale, it made Francis Peck subtitle his *Antiquarian Annals of Stanford* of 1727 *Academia Tercia Anglicana,* or 'The Third English University', and it fuelled the fertile minds of William Stukeley and later Victorian romantics.

Finally, Stamford put itself forward in the 1960s as one of the sites for the new generation of universities, citing the town's 'university history' in support of its case. The idea had been put forward as early as the end of the Second World War, when E. M. W. Tillyard had advocated a new relief university for Oxford and Cambridge at Stamford. Following the foundation of new universities at such places as York and Lancaster, hopes for a university at Stamford ran high. A two hundred acre site along Tinwell Road was suggested with plots of land in the centre of the town reserved for halls of residence. J. M. Lee in his essay 'Modern Stamford' published in *The Making of Stamford* says, 'A real university, if it came, would at least release Stamford from a fate which for such a long time remained a burden upon its political development, that the borough, as the guide books would say "is only of historical interest."' But in 1965, it was announced that no new university would be built for ten years and that priority would go to the expansion of existing universities. This, and the growth of student unrest, finally killed off all hopes of establishing a university in the town.

QUEEN BOADICEA
& THE ROMAN TOWN AT STAMFORD

The *Legend*

HEN THE Romans built Ermine Street, their great road from the south coast to the Humber, they deliberately aligned it close to the ancient university town of Stamford, then called *Doorebriff*. At this strategic river crossing they established a town called *Durobrivae*, from which the Saxon word 'Welland' later derived, meaning '*raging, boiling, bubbling*'. The site of this settlement was in Bredcroft or 'Bradcroft' meadow, and in the nineteenth century there was still evidence of its existence. Samuel Sharp writing in 1847 says: 'There is evidence... of its having been a Roman settlement in the time of Agricola, and that his legions established here a permanent encampment, the remains of which are clearly traceable even to the present day.' There was also a smaller walled town two miles to the north called *Gausennae* at what is now Great Casterton, which acted as an extra garrison.

In A.D. 61 the settlement was brutally destroyed by the illustrious Queen Boadicea, leader of the Iceni tribe of the Norfolk area. She had defeated the Roman IX Legion at a bloody battle in the Godmanchester area (Cambridgeshire) and pursued the survivors along Ermine Street to their base at Lincoln. Boadicea, on her shining chariot with scythes on the wheels, razed all the Roman settlements in her path, and so *Durobrivae* was obliterated. There is a monument in Bredcroft meadow in memory of this remarkable event in Stamford's history.

QUEEN BOADICEA
AD 61

Commentary

The siting of the Roman Ermine Street just to the west of Stamford prompted Francis Peck in 1727 to suggest that Stamford was formerly the important Roman town of *Durobrivae*, originally called *Doorebriff*. He supported the claim with some incoherent etymology that related the name to the Saxon word 'Welland', irrespective of the fact that the gentle Welland does not rage or boil (according to Ekwall's *English River Names*, Welland means 'good stream'). *Durobrivae* actually means 'bridge-fort' and was situated ten miles south-east of Stamford on the River Nene at Water Newton.

It appears the Romans had no defensive position on the Welland and the earliest settlement in the area was the Roman camp on the River Gwash at what is now Great Casterton. A deep defensive ditch still survives there, but it was only a small settlement and Camden's 'town' of *Gausennae* is probably *Causennis* which stood further to the north on the River Witham. Only small Roman fragments have been found in Stamford - Sharp's 'clearly traceable' Roman camp which apparently stood one furlong north-west of the town is untraceable - but there is the site of a villa just to the west of the town. It has been suggested that the Bredcroft site might have been a small sub-Roman settlement in the period between the decline of Great Casterton and the growth of Stamford. Popular etymology has claimed that 'Bredcroft' was the place where the town's medieval bakers kept their ovens and Burton claims there was a court house there, but there is no evidence. The land was owned by Queen Edith and was situated in Rutland outside the Borough of Stamford.

The Boudicca tale is based on a statement by the contemporary Roman historian, Tacitus, that after his defeat, Petilius Cerialis, the commander of the IX Legion, escaped with his cavalry 'and found shelter behind the defences of [their] camp'. This does not necessarily imply a chase and no evidence of an attack was found when the Roman town at Casterton was excavated in the 1950s. The whole connection is so slight that the legend only appears in tourist-orientated guide books of the twentieth century. It was given enough credence in the 1960s, though for a monument to be erected by the Roman ford in Bredcroft meadow recording her chase. Professor W. F. Grimes in his essay 'The Archaeology of the Stamford Region' in *The Making of Stamford* suggests that 'the inscription on the recently erected pillar that marks the Roman crossing on the Welland ought to be replaced by one which does less violence to the facts as they appear to be.'

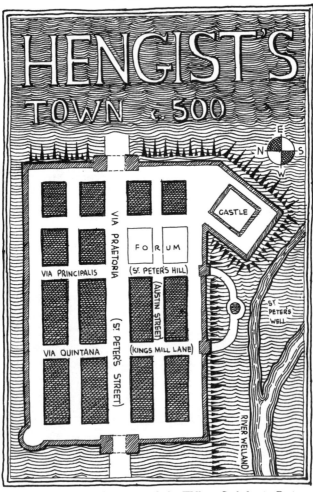

Hengist's town based on a drawing made by William Stukeley in *Designs*, 1736.

THE
BATTLE OF STAMFORD
& HENGIST'S TOWN

I see evidently thro' the obscure mist of past ages that Hengist our great
Saxon progenitor, is Founder of Stamford.
William Stukeley, *Diaries*, 1735.

The *Legend*

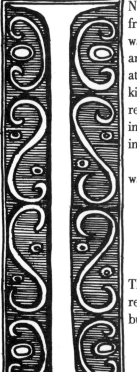

N THE early fifth century, England was under attack
from invading tribes of Picts and Scots. They had laid
waste the entire north of the country and in 449 they
arrived at the university town of Stamford. In a last
attempt to crush the invasion, Vortigern, the British
king, enlisted the help of the Saxon army under the
renowned general, Hengist. But by inviting the Saxons
into the country he planted the seed for a new
invasion upon his soil.

Hengist's army met the Scots at Stamford, which
was now in a ruinous state;

> The enemies were come unto Stamford: where when
> the Picts and Scots used long lances and spears, the
> Saxons fought with swords and axes.
> **Ranulf Higden,** *Polychronicon, c.*1352

The Saxon forces scored a significant victory and in
return Vortigern gave Hengist land in Stamford to
build the first Saxon town in Britain. Camden adds:

> Gausennae [as he calls the Roman town at Great
> Casterton] ..was destroyed, when...the Picts and Scots
> had laid waste all the country as far as Stamford... I
> should think that Stamford sprang from this town.

Hengist chose a site just to the west of the existing settlement on an elevated position and constructed a Roman-style town based on knowledge gained whilst serving in the Roman army. The structured grid layout of this town can still be traced today in the St. Peter's area of Stamford. St. Peter's Street was formerly the axial *Via Praetoria* with the *forum*, or market place, on the site of St. Peter's Church. The castle stood to the south-east by the river and the whole town was heavily fortified, surviving until the Danish attacks in the ninth century.

After completing the magnificent castle, Hengist began plotting his mastery of the kingdom. Stukeley in his diary tells us how he invited King Vortigern to be entertained there and on the king's arrival he introduced him to Rowena, his beautiful daughter, who presented Vortigern with a gold wassail cup. Vortigern was so taken by her charms that he took her for his wife. In return he gave Hengist land in Kent where Hengist's descendants ruled until the late eighth century (the 'Oescinga' dynasty).

Anglo-Saxon battle based on drawing in the *Canterbury Hexateuch*.

Commentary

The story of Hengist in Stamford is a local legend based on a reference to a battle at Stamford in Henry of Huntingdon's (1084-1155) *Historia Anglorum*. This implies a local tradition already current in the twelfth century and might be based on a lost source. Gildas writing in the mid-sixth century gives no details of the battle and Bede in 731 mentions Vortigern and Hengist but does not specify any location. Geoffrey of Monmouth began the Hengist in Lincolnshire legend by stating that Hengist was granted land in Lindsey, in Lincolnshire, where he built a fortress called *Thranceastre* which was later associated with Castor. Bede merely states that Hengist was granted a settlement in the east of the country which was probably in Kent where Hengist founded a royal dynasty.

William Stukeley further elaborated the legend in the eighteenth century when he proposed that the St. Peter's area of Stamford was the site of Hengist's town, despite the fact that Stamford has never been in Lindsey. This shows Stukeley's keen topographical eye and fanciful imagination, but whilst the St. Peter's area is one of the oldest places of settlement and has a regularised street pattern, like the rest of the town it does not predate the ninth century. The account of Vortigern's marriage to Hengist's daughter is first mentioned in the early ninth century *Historia Brittonum*, formerly attributed to Nennius (where however Rowena is not named). It was filled-out and popularised by Geoffrey of Monmouth and was simply incorporated into the Stamford legend by Stukeley.

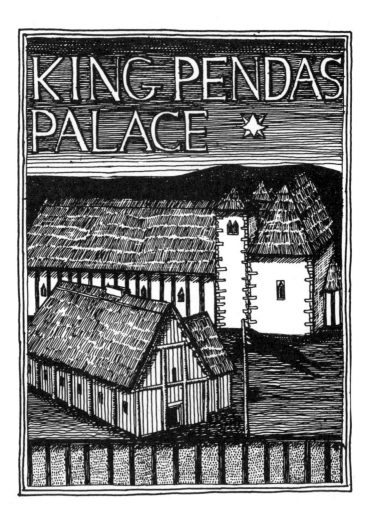

STAMFORD
AS THE SEAT OF THE
MERCIAN GOVERNMENT
& the *Foundation of St. Leonard's Priory*

The *Myth*

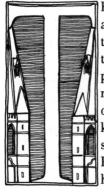

HE IMPORTANCE of Hengist's Saxon town and the ancient university made Stamford the ideal location for the siting of the Mercian court and government. The town was not liable to attack owing to its geographical position and extensive fortifications and it was situated near the Fens from which the word 'Mercia' originated. Stamford became the capital of a huge kingdom extending right across central England (it is still referred to as the capital of the Fens) and King Penda (c.577-655), the last pagan King of Mercia, had his palace here.

In 658 King Alchfrith of Northumbria held his court at Stamford and he granted St. Wilfrid, later bishop of York, land to found a monastery in the town. By the Welland St. Wilfrid built St. Leonard's Priory, a masterpiece of Anglo-Saxon architecture, befitting its status as the first religious house in all Mercia. Samuel Sharp tells us that on Wilfrid's death the monks of the priory helped to carry his body from Oundle in Northamptonshire to Ripon Abbey, where he was buried. This beautiful priory of St. Leonard's, originally belonging to the Holy Isle of Lindisfarne, was later destroyed by marauding Danes and was only rebuilt in 1082 with the co-operation of William the Conqueror. According to Arthur Mee, the new priory was designed by William Carileff, the great Norman architect of Durham Cathedral.

King Alchfrith also built St. Peter's church which was the first church in Stamford and all Mercia. It was built on the site of the *forum* of Hengist's Roman-style town in front of the great castle. Writing in his diary, William Stukeley takes his friend 'Panagius' to see a supposed doorway of it. Panagius modestly declares:

> Hail noble fragment of antiquity: first fruit of royal Alkfrid's [Alchfrith's] pious zeal! This was the real gate of Heaven on Earth; founded in holy, and just principles of true religion, pure Christianity. Where like the hart thirsting for liquid streams, the soul wing'd with devotions rapturous flame, pants and aspires to thee O Good Supreme!

Commentary

The whole legend starts from a misinterpretation by John Wessington, Prior of Durham (1416-46), of Bede's eighth-century account of King Alchfrith granting Wilfrid land in 'Stanford' and a monastery in Ripon. Although Wilfrid did evangelise Mercia and founded a site at Oundle in Northamptonshire, it is probable the reference is to another Stamford, as the name was not uncommon and Alchfrith is unlikely to have owned any land in this area. There is no mention of a monastery and it is likely the Ripon reference has been confused with the 'Stanford' entry. The 1082 connection is also spurious and the first mention of the Priory is in 1146, implying it was founded by Durham at the beginning of the twelfth century. The surviving structure also dates from that time.

The idea that Stamford was the centre of Mercian government was invented by William Stukeley in the 1730s from his belief that Alchfrith had held his court here and that it had formerly been Hengist's town. The concept of a centre of government in early Anglo-Saxon England, though, is nonsense as the king would travel around his kingdom, and where the king was, the government was. The term 'Mercia' actually derives from 'Mercians', meaning 'Border-folk'.

As for St. Peter's church, it was probably the 'mother church' of Stamford, and is mentioned in Domesday. It could date back as far as the middle of the ninth century and was closely associated with the later castle. The church belonged to the royal church at Hambleton and served the queen's estates in Stamford. It closed in the mid-sixteenth century.

ROGER BACON
AND THE
BRAZENOSE HEAD
The *Myth*

RIAR Roger Bacon, the renowned thirteenth-century philosopher and scientist, known as 'the wonderful doctor', worked for many years at Stamford University, being a Fellow of Brazenose College on St. Paul's Street. Whilst pondering on the history of the town and how often it had been conquered and invaded, he struck upon the idea of fashioning a wonderful head of brass that could speak and was omniscient. This head would have the ability to tell Bacon where the necessary resources were to build a wall of brass around Stamford, 'that is, the most powerful defence and strongest fortification that gold could have effected' (Thomas Browne). Bacon was an acclaimed alchemist and necromancer but he had to enlist the help of his friend Friar Bungay to assist in making this remarkable head. They consulted their guardian demon, who was under their power, and were informed of a secret process lasting one month after which time the head would speak. After considerable labour the brazen head was finished and attached to the door of the college (which still survives). Bacon and Bungay were so exhausted that they set their servant, Miles, to watch it whilst they were asleep, under the instruction that they should be woken if the head started speaking.

Miles kept vigil by the door but began to grow tired. Suddenly the head spoke, saying 'Time is', but Miles considered this unimportant and ignored it. It spoke again saying 'Time was' and still Miles refused to wake his masters. Finally the head roared 'Time's past', whereupon it fell to the floor with a tremendous noise and shattered into a thousand pieces. The great noise woke Bacon and he hurried to the college gate

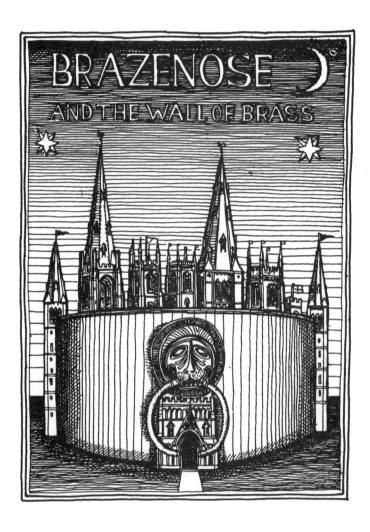

only to find that the opportunity to build the wall of brass around Stamford had been missed and all his work was undone.

Commentary

The bizarre dream-like tale of Roger Bacon's brazen head first appeared in the late medieval period and was a popular romantic fable tacked onto Bacon's life story. No location is given for the event and the original tale concerns the defence of the country and the erection of a brass wall around the whole of England. It is frequently mentioned in literature, in particular Robert Greene's *Honourable History of Roger Bacon and Friar Bungay* of 1594, but modern accounts of his life simply ignore it. Thomas Browne, the seventeenth-century physician and author, believed it to be a misunderstanding caused by an alchemical description that had been too literally interpreted. His explanation, though, being also in the deliberately obscure jargon of alchemy, is surely itself a subject for misunderstanding:

> Implying no more by the copper head, than the vessel wherein it was wrought; and by the words it spake, the opportunity to be watched, about the tempus ortus, or birth of the mystical child, or philosophical king of Lullius: the rising of the terra foliata of Arnoldus, when the earth sufficiently impregnated with the water, ascendeth white and splendent; which not observed the work is irrecoverably lost.

Its association with Stamford is connected with the legend of the medieval university and the name of Brazenose, which was linked to the 'brazen head' and Oxford University where Bacon really worked. The story was certainly a common tradition by Peck's time and he says,

> I have seen some wiseacres [fools], when others told this, shake their heads merely out of a concern, that the man should be so careless as to miss the opportunity!

The tale, therefore, was simply adopted into the mythology of the town and adapted to suit its new home. The brazen head became the

Brazen-nofe College Gate at Stanford.

Reproduced from Francis Peck's *Annals*, 1727

door knocker on the Brazenose gate on St. Paul's Street, in spite of the fact that it was supposed to have shattered to pieces. The story was also altered so that the servant had to remove the iron ring from its mouth, whereby the town would be walled around with brass. A local attempt at an interpretation of it appears in George Burton's *Guide to Stamford and Neighbourhood*. He states that an expert on ancient British dialects considered the wall of brass to be a confusion with an old tradition that if the ring of sluices and embankments which Bladud erected around the 'brazen' waters of the Fenland were broken by flood, then Stamford would be surrounded by 'brayes' or shallow stretches of water! This explanation, though, considering that the story originally never related to Stamford, is even more bizarre than Thomas Browne's.

ST. THOMAS
STAMFORD'S LOST CHURCH
The *Myth*

TAMFORD is usually referred to as having fourteen churches in the medieval period, but at one time there was a fifteenth, dedicated to St. Thomas. Its location has been the cause of much dispute because the church was brutally destroyed by the Lancastrian army in their sack of the town in 1461. It probably stood either in Rock Close (the triangle of land off Scotgate and Empingham Road) or on the site of Rock House, opposite. Medieval burials were discovered on the Rock Close site in 1816, and also on the Rock House site in recent times. An article in the *Stamford Mercury* on 28 December 1950 claimed that St. Thomas' Church was where Queen Eleanor's funeral cortege stayed the night in December 1290 whilst on its journey to Westminster. This was why Stamford's Eleanor Cross was later erected at the junction of Empingham and Casterton Roads. William Stukeley, though, considered the church to be situated on the north side of All Saints Street and he drew a sketch of a fifteenth-century door which survived at that time.

Decoration from Francis Peck's *Annals*, 1727.

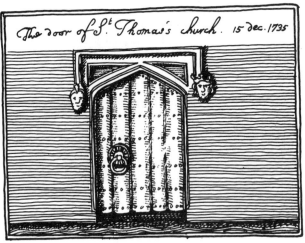

The door of St. Thomas's church. 15 Dec. 1735

St. Thomas' door from a drawing by William Stukeley, 1735.

Commentary

Richard Butcher writing in 1646 is the first to mention St. Thomas' church, for medieval bishops' registers show quite clearly that it never existed. The myth was probably sparked off by the existence of a St. Thomas' Lane and Well in the town (locations now unknown), the St. Thomas' chapel in All Saints' church, and the Hospital of St. Thomas and St. John (now Lord Burghley's Almshouses), which apparently had a chapel over the bridge. Stukeley is the first to give it a definite site and the discovery of skeletons in Rock Close in 1816 encouraged Drakard in his *History of Stamford* to give this as its position. This view was then copied by later writers. The skeletons found on this site were buried in unorthodox manner and might have been plague victims. More skeletons of probable plague victims were uncovered on the Rock House site in July 1987. The *Mercury* article is a fiction inspired by the erroneous belief that the Eleanor Cross stood at this position. Eyewitness accounts and Stukeley's excavation of the base of the cross in 1745 indicates that it stood about half-a-mile up Casterton Road on the brow into Foxdale.

THE LANCASTRIAN SACK

O F

STAMFORD IN 1461

'An epoch in the town's history'

With what disasters it was then turmoyl'd,
By hereticks undone, by Danes much sackt and spoyl'd
Yet at the length her ruines were redrest,
By kings & friends; her enimies supprest:
In strength and state, with walls & castle proud,
With grants & privledges great endow'd,
She flourish'd under governours discreet
Till the whole land with civil warres did meet;
When York & Lancaster their swords out drewe,
And, like mad lyons keene, their kindred slew.
The northerne soulders all with rage incenst,
With quenchless flames then Stamford's glory quencht.
Who never since her towring crest could raise
To former greatnesse, as in former dayes.
Richard Butcher, 1646.

The *Legend*

N 1363 the manor of Stamford became the property of the Dukes of York. The town remained prosperous and pledged its loyalty to its new owner in a rebellion against the Lancastrian government in 1452. The price for such loyalty, though, was high and Stamford was later ruined during the Wars of the Roses. It never again recovered its former glory.

The Lancastrian army arrived at Stamford in February 1461, on their march to St. Albans, and were led by Henry VI's French consort, Queen Margaret. The townspeople were prepared. They manned the towers and bastions and the great gates were shut fast. But the

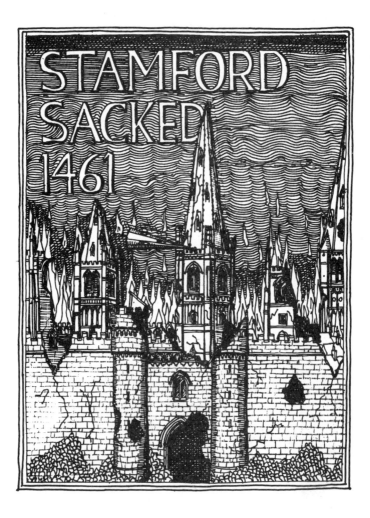

Lancastrian army proved too powerful, and after a brave fight the defences were breached. The town was plundered and destroyed, together with 'many writings of their antiquities and privleges' (Leland).

Bentley Wood, writing in 1889, pictured the terrible scene:

> They fired the sacred edifices... and there was heard the dismal din of metal as the flames, mounting from storey to storey, at last set free the quivering bells. Seven of our sixteen churches were thus reduced to ruins whilst the others were more or less damaged.

Camden writing in the late sixteenth century states they 'destroyed everything with fire and sword: Nor could it ever after recover its ancient dignity'.

After the sack only the six principal churches were rebuilt. E. W. Lovegrove in an essay on the churches of Stamford in 1908 says that St. John's and St. Martin's were in so ruinous a state that completely new Perpendicular style buildings had to be erected on their site. The others, particularly All Saints' and St. Mary's, were extensively rebuilt using the materials of the poorer churches. Thus one of England's greatest medieval towns was destroyed, its churches shattered, and its houses razed. Bentley Wood says: 'never, although four centuries have elapsed since this fateful day, has Stamford recovered from the effects of February 1461'.

Despite this bitter tragedy the town again rallied itself to the Yorkist cause when in 1470 they assisted King Edward IV in dispelling a Lancastrian uprising at the battle of Loosecoat Field. In return for this support the king granted Stamford the permission to use the royal coat of arms on the borough shield. Butcher says:

> The Coat of arms depicted on our shield
> Was honourably won at Loosecoat field....
> And next to honour Stamford for such aid,
> His own paternall armes to it convey'd,
> Joyn'd with Earl Warren's shield of high renown,
> Who was formerly owner of this towne.

Reproduced from 2nd edition of Richard Butcher's *Survey*, 1717.

Commentary

The circumstances of the sack of Stamford are true but the seriousness and implications of the event have been greatly exaggerated. The sixteenth-century historians misinterpreted the decayed state of the town, caused by the collapse of the wool trade and the dissolution of the monasteries, as the lingering results of the sack. This was taken up by local historians as an opportunity to highlight the indignity committed against the town and to use that as an excuse for Stamford's embarrassing decline into a small provincial town - the 'sleepy hollow' backwater of the nineteenth century.

An examination of the facts soon reveals inconsistencies in the story. The town's smaller churches had either already disappeared by 1461 (All Saints' beyond the Bridge, St. Mary Bynwerk and St. Michael at Cornstall), or they continued up until the mid-sixteenth century (St. Stephen, St. Andrew, St. Peter and St. Clement). Windows are usually the first things to go in a riot, but medieval glass survived in many of the churches - in St. George's and St. Martin's, for example - and Yorkist symbols remained in the windows of St. Mary's. St. John's was in fact rebuilt ten years before the sack, but it survived remarkably well, and its stained glass existed up until the eighteenth century when Stukeley records its removal. St. Martin's was rebuilt over twenty years after the sack, which implies there was no extensive damage to its structure, and although All Saints' was also rebuilt at this time, a great deal of its thirteenth-century architecture survived. As for the records being destroyed, it is true nothing now predates 1465, but early records certainly existed up until the early seventeenth century.

Shortly after the sack, Stamford was granted its great Charter of Incorporation by the newly acclaimed Yorkist king Edward IV, which gave it considerable rewards for its loyalty (an earlier charter of 972, which was a post-conquest forgery, and only referred to the mint at Stamford, was still celebrated in 1972). This 1463 charter is the more probable origin for the use of the royal arms on the borough shield and Butcher's account of Loosecoat field is more heroic than historical. However, the real facts of the battle are still interesting.

The battle was instigated by a Lancastrian uprising led by Sir Robert Welles and supported by Richard Neville, the Earl of Warwick. King Edward came to Stamford and summoned Sir Robert's father, Lord Welles, and the King's Champion, Sir Thomas Dymock, to appear before him. When Sir Robert refused to disperse his forces, both men were executed. The king's army was dispatched and met the rebels at a site now known as 'Bloody Oaks', about five miles north-west of the town near Empingham. There was hardly a battle, though, for when the king's artillery fired, the Lancastrians fled, apparently throwing aside their coats to aid their retreat, thereby giving the battle its name. Robert Welles was captured and beheaded.

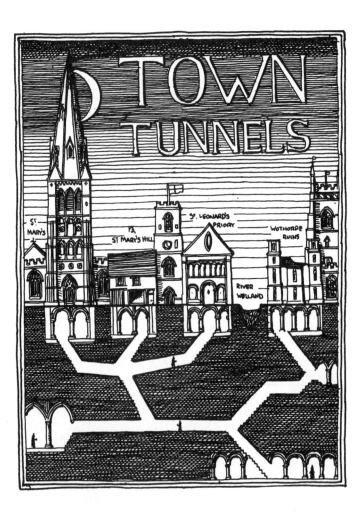

TOWN TUNNELS

In the many religious houses the inmates were some engaged in removing their sacred vessels and relics into their secret chambers, or building them up in subterranean passages which undermined the town.
E. Bentley Wood, *1461, an Epoch in the History of Stamford*, 1889.

The *Myth*

ANY ANCIENT towns in England were originally built with a network of underground tunnels connecting the sites of the churches, guildhalls, monasteries and nunneries. These were used as retreats in times of attack and for clandestine communication between the religious houses. Anne Pennick in an essay on the tunnels of Glastonbury claims that larger tunnels follow ley lines (originally straight alignments of assorted ancient historic sites, now credited to be on lines of mystic energy), and that they reflect the 'mystery and sanctity attaching to places of paramount geomantic importance in the topographical interrelation of religious sites'.

Stamford is reputed to have several ancient tunnels, although after the Dissolution in 1539 many of them were either destroyed or blocked off. One runs from Wothorpe Priory (now the site of Wothorpe ruins) to St. Michael's Nunnery and under the river to St. Leonard's Priory and the Greyfriars site (now the Hospital). Others run from the crypt at 13 St. Mary's Hill to St. Mary's Church and the Town Hall, and there are numerous tunnels under most of the central medieval streets.

Commentary

The secret underground passage has a special place in the imagination of the English people. The romantic fantasy is nurtured in our youth with Enid Blyton books and ghost stories and manifests itself in the invention of tunnel myths. Unfortunately there is no historical or archaeological evidence for any tunnels under Stamford, nor under any medieval town. Monasteries and nunneries were

51

relatively safe from attack until the Dissolution and would have no need for elaborate and impractical tunnels. Also, the marshy ground near rivers, where most towns are sited, is ill-suited for tunnel construction.

The myth is perpetuated by many factors. The popular, but false, belief that a pointed or Gothic arch means that a building was originally ecclesiastical is enough to kindle a story. The pointed arch was merely the most efficient form of building technology at the time (in Stamford a pointed arch is sometimes used in medieval cellars to span the sites of earlier quarry pits) and the undercroft at no. 13 St. Mary's Hill was not a crypt for St. Mary's Church, but a shop with steps giving access to the street. Later eighteenth and nineteenth-century cellars are prime candidates for tunnel status; they are usually stone built in the form of barrel vaults which give the end walls the appearance of plugs which seal off long tunnels - a common feature of such myths. River conduits and drains are also mistaken for tunnels. During the St. Leonard's excavation, the reredorter (toilet) drain was uncovered which entered into a fissure for drainage to the river. This sparked off talk of a tunnel leading to Burghley House where a mythical monastery founded in 1158 by William Waterville was supposed to have stood (this monastery is still cited in the Burghley House guide book).

These 'tunnels' are made to connect with sites of current or popular importance. The medieval undercroft under no. 13 St. Mary's Hill is just one of five in the town, but is singled out because of its notoriety. Wothorpe House, because of its ruinous state, its unusual design and its proximity to the site of Wothorpe nunnery, is also a victim of such mythology, but it was merely a dower house for widows of the earls and marquesses at Burghley. Burghley itself is given importance because of its size and its 'monastery'.

Despite the lack of *any* evidence the tunnel myth has a lively oral tradition and is still widely believed. When an academic approach is used the theory begins to crumble. Anne Pennick's essay on Glastonbury produces no convincing evidence at all, yet concludes that there is 'a vast subterranean complex beneath Glastonbury, as befits a place of such ecumenical and mythological

52

complexity'. Evidently the tunnel myth is still firmly in the popular psyche of today.

There have been natural caverns or fissures discovered under Stamford, but there is no evidence to suggest they were ever used by man. In 1847 during the construction of the Midland Railway a cavern was found underneath St. Martin's, fifteen feet below the ground and thirty feet long. In 1865 another chamber was uncovered near the site of St. Mary Bynwerk off St. Peter's Street, seven feet below ground and twenty-six feet by seventeen feet. The *Stamford Mercury* believed them both to be places of religious refuge!

OLIVER CROMWELL,
THE SIEGE OF BURGHLEY HOUSE & THE
CAPTURE OF STAMFORD
The *Legend*

URING THE Civil War Stamford's ancient monuments were defaced and vandalised and the whole town was almost burnt to the ground for its Royalist sympathies. Oliver Cromwell came to Stamford in 1643, following the retreat of the Cavalier army who had tried to capture Peterborough. The Cavaliers occupied Burghley House, but they were heavily outnumbered, and Cromwell forced them to surrender after a bitter siege. He then ordered that the house be destroyed. It was only after a passionate entreaty by his relative Lady Frances Wingfield, who lived in St. Martin's, that Cromwell relented and he later presented the widowed countess of Burghley with a portrait of himself.

What would now be the fate of Stamford, always the faithful supporter of the king; would the pillage and devastation of 1461 be repeated, and the

53

town, which was gradually recovering from the disaster of the Roses, be again reduced to wreck and ruin?'
Bentley Wood from article in the *Stamford News*, collected in his scrapbooks.

During the siege Stamford had rung its church bells backwards in order to summon Royalist support and in response Cromwell threatened to raze the entire town. Lady Wingfield again interceded and as Bentley Wood says 'a woman's argument was too much for him, and he gave way'. The town was captured instead, but not without loss. The beautiful thirteenth-century Eleanor Cross was hacked to pieces and James Hissey in *Over Fen and Wold* of 1898 says 'Shame to those savages of the Great Rebellion who swept away the very foundations of it.' In Broad Street the ancient Market Cross was likewise destroyed.

Reproduced from 2nd edition of Francis Peck's *Desiderata Curiosa*, 1779.

Commentary

Oliver Cromwell has been accused of vandalising many of the ancient treasures of England's towns, but he has become the victim of legend. He has become a scapegoat and an excuse, so that romantic writers can maintain their vision of a lost golden age. Mackenzie Walcott lamented 'it is almost inconceivable the waste that has mercilessly made havoc of the ancient Memorials that gave renown to Stamford'.

The siege of Burghley House is well documented by a member of Cromwell's army, but there is no mention of any threatened destruction of the house or the town - which was apparently taken with little resistance - nor of the intercession of Lady Wingfield. There is also no evidence to suggest that the crosses were destroyed by Cromwell, and Butcher states that the Eleanor Cross was still standing in 1645.

KING CHARLES I's
LAST DAYS OF FREEDOM

Thou passedst through this gate, self ruled as yet
Though king no longer, ere another night
A captive, shortly through that other gate
Hunted by human judges blind with wrath
'Fore an all comprehending Judge divine.
Rev. Claude Tickell, 1906.

The *Legend*

 ING CHARLES I spent his last days and very last night as a free man in Stamford at the house of Alderman Richard Wolph in Barn Hill (on the site of the present Stukeley House). The king, who was disguised as a servant to escape Cromwell's army, was accompanied by his personal chaplain, Michael Hudson, rector of Uffington near Stamford, and Mr. Ashburnham.

On May 3rd 1646 they arrived at the town by a devious route from Melton Mowbray, and entered the house through the postern gate in the old town wall, which was later rebuilt by William Stukeley. The king was the guest of Richard Wolph, a prosperous gentleman farmer, until the evening of May 4th, when he left by the same gate for Southwell. Apparently he repeatedly climbed the town wall during his stay to watch for his pursuers. On arriving at Southwell, Charles handed

55

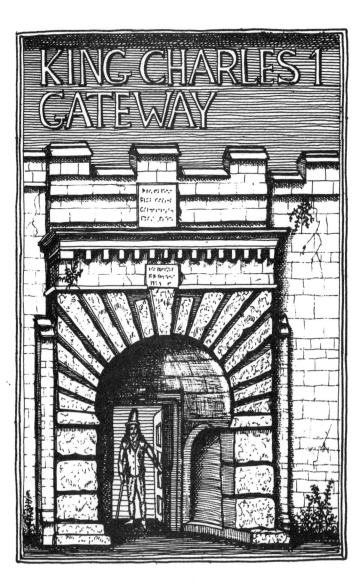

himself over to the Scottish commissioners in expectation of their support, but negotiations between them collapsed, and the Scots sold him to Parliament for £400,000.

Commentary

The tale is told in some detail by William Stukeley in a letter to Noah Curtis of Woolsthorpe dated 1746 and is reproduced in Drakard's *History of Stamford*. Stukeley lived in the house where the king is supposed to have stayed and his fertility of imagination and lack of sources encourage suspicion. Neither the later edition of Butcher, which contains a few additions, nor Howgrave nor Peck make any reference to the incident. In Peck's *Desiderata Curiosa* of 1735, there is a transcript of an examination of John Browne of St. Ives, who was involved in the royalist escape. He says the king 'lodged at a gentleman's house in Stamford whose name the examinant knows not'. Stukeley, therefore, appears to be the first person to identify the house, but he supplies no evidence for his claim. S. R. Gardiner in his *History of the Great Civil War* merely says, '...he arrived at Stamford on the evening of the 3rd. The next day he kept himself concealed, and then, after travelling all night, alighted at seven in the morning of May 5 at Montreuil's lodgings in Southwell.' This also suggests that Charles did not spend his very last night of freedom at Stamford as is claimed.

T H E
STAMFORD MERCURY
BRITAIN'S OLDEST NEWSPAPER

Cradled in the lap of the Bloodless Revolution and reared on the freedom of the press granted by William III.
Harold Evans, editor, 1920-1950.

The *Myth*

IN 1826, Richard Newcomb, the proprietor of the *Stamford Mercury*, announced that his newspaper was the earliest provincial paper ever published in Britain. His calculations, based on the paper's numerical sequence, showed that it was first printed in February 1695, by William Thompson and Francis Bailey. This was just after the Licensing Act was repealed, which had previously confined printers to London, York, and Oxford and Cambridge Universities. This meant that the *Mercury* was the first newspaper to be published outside those places.

Commentary

Newcomb's claim was based purely on his assertion that Thompson and Bailey's newspaper ran for 'nearly forty years' prior to Francis Howgrave's take-over in 1732. It was not substantiated by any evidence and William Thompson was only fifteen years old in 1695. Bailey and Thompson, in fact, founded the *Stamford Poste* newspaper in 1710 and after the Stamp Act of 1712, which placed duty on newspapers, it was reduced to pamphlet size and renamed the *Stamford Mercury*. The 1695 date was possibly invented by Newcomb to goad his arch-rival John Drakard, who ran the radical *Stamford News* from 1809 to 1834, as Newcomb was well aware of the 1712 date. Newcomb fought a duel with Octavius Gilchrist, the editor of the *News*, sued Drakard for libel, interfered with his business tenancy and later bought Drakard's house, which he pulled down to build his own pretentious Rock House.

As for being the oldest surviving newspaper, this claim is invalidated by the *Worcester Post Man* founded in 1709. However, as the *Worcester Post Man* has changed its title to the *Worcester Journal*, the *Mercury* could claim to be the oldest surviving newspaper with the same name.

MIRACLES
AND OTHER
SUPERNATURAL
TALES

N THIS section religious medieval miracles have been incorporated with later supernatural traditions. Both have a common theme in that they occur within human experience but involve some fantastic happening that is not quite of this world. They are presented here in chronological order and mostly without comment, as their very specific and often personal nature makes them impossible to qualify.

HEREWARD THE WAKE
& THE WOLF

THIS TALE is taken from the twelfth-century *De Gestis Herwardi Saxonis*, which tells the story of Hereward, an eleventh-century rebel who opposed the Norman invaders in the Fenlands. The story of Hereward was later popularised by the novelist Charles Kingsley (1819-1875), who lived for some years at Barnack Rectory, about four miles to the south-east of Stamford.

After sacking Peterborough, following a dispute with the abbey, Hereward set off with his men in the direction of Stamford. During the night a storm descended upon them and they became lost in the dense woodland. Just as they were about to give up hope of finding their way a huge white wolf appeared, which instead of attacking them began to guide them skilfully through the dark wood. Flames appeared on the soldiers' lances like "fairies' lights" illuminating their path, and they remained lit despite the heavy rain. When they had got beyond Stamford and to their destination, the wolf suddenly disappeared and the flames on the lances were extinguished.

INGULPH
& THE BAILIFF

THIS STORY appears to be told by Ingulph, Abbot of Crowland Abbey, 1075-1109, in his *Crowland History*. The book is in fact a fourteenth or fifteenth-century forgery of uncertain Crowland authorship, but it is probably based partly on authentic contemporary evidence.

The story concerns Crowland's bailiff, Ashford of Helpstone, who in 1076 was summoned by Ingulph before the King's Justices at Stamford for trying to extort land from the abbey. On his way there he was thrown from his horse and killed. As his relations carried him off to be buried, the sky suddenly darkened and the heavens opened. As the storm raged about them, the bier unaccountably broke and the corpse tumbled into a meadow the bailiff had been trying to extort. At that very moment Ingulph came by and on seeing him Ashford's relations acknowledged God's judgement in favour of the abbey. Justin Simpson, in his *Historical Sketches* in the *Stamford Mercury* written in the late nineteenth century, reflects that 'such a satisfactory and speedy termination to a law suit rarely falls to the lot of man to witness in these degenerate days'.

THE BLACK HUNTERS
OF BURGHLEY

 HIS TALE is recorded in *The Anglo-Saxon Chronicle* and in the twelfth-century chronicle of Hugh Candidus of Peterborough.

After the appointment of Henry of Poitou, a self-seeking Norman, to the abbacy of Peterborough in 1127, the woods from that place to Stamford became full of strange huntsmen,

> black, huge and hideous, who rode on black horses and on he-goats, and their hounds were jet black, with eyes like saucers..

Many monks and local people heard the dreadful cry of horns and Hugh Candidus tells us 'a great many persons, of unquestionable veracity, both saw these hunters and heard them'.

61

The ghost-huntsmen tradition was one of the central images of northern mythology and was symbolic of the presence of dark or evil forces, connected here with the appointment of an unpopular abbot. In Jakob Grimm's *Teutonic Mythology*, it is suggested that the tradition originated from Woden or Odin, the principal god of Germanic pagan religion, but the image also has parallels with the four horsemen of the biblical apocalypse. Its inclusion in *The Anglo-Saxon Chronicle* is an important and very early reference to the tradition. Peck, though, dismisses the event as 'humour' and Justin Simpson comments: 'If this fable was trustworthy we could scarcely do otherwise than believe that not only was Stamford in days past frequently honoured by the presence of English Kings and Queens, but also that His Satanic Majesty occasionally hunted in the neighbourhood.'

GILBERT OF SEMPRINGHAM
AND THE
WONDERFUL PREGNANCY

IN THE *The Book of St. Gilbert, pp. 112-115,* the following miracle is reported of this twelfth-century saint:

> A man from Stamford had lived a long time with his wife without having children. It happened that Father Gilbert stopped at their house to spend the night. The discreet lady of the household put her trust in the holiness of the guest she had received, and prepared a place for him on her own couch so that through his merits she might be found worthy to bear a son, as the Shunammite did through Elisha. It turned out just as she believed. For when her husband came home to sleep he before long fathered a son upon her, and they named him after Father Gilbert. When Our Lord's servant heard what had happened, being a cheerful and generous person he sent the boy a cow to supply him with food, acting just as if the boy had been his own son.

Our more cynical age, though, might suspect that Gilbert's generosity was motivated by more than spiritual interest in the boy's welfare!

HUGH OF LINCOLN
& THE SHOEMAKER

THE MIRACLES surrounding the funeral procession of Hugh of
Lincoln are taken from the *Flores Historiarum*, a thirteenth and
fourteenth-century text originally credited to Matthew of Westminster (it
was actually written by the monks of St. Albans and Westminster), and
from the *Nova Legenda Angliae* by John Capgrave (1393-1464).

Hugh of Lincoln died in London in November 1200 and on the way back to Lincoln the funeral procession passed through Stamford. Bentley Wood in an article in the *Stamford Post* in 1900 sets the scene:

> As the funeral train approached the town numerous people went out to meet it, regardless of the boisterous inclemency of the weather; the bells were tolled from the churches and monasteries: shutters and blinds were closed on every hand in token of mourning. Slowly it drew near, the quaint plain-song dirges and requiems of the monks sounding still more weird to the accompaniment of the howling wind. The long tapers carried around the hearse burnt freely in spite of the gale and the torrents of rain, and cast a lurid unnatural light on the sombre gathering as it threaded its way through the dark cheerless streets.

One of the faithful who braved the weather was a shoemaker, known in the town for his unusual devotion. When the cortege stopped he bowed his head under the bier and prayed requesting that he should die that night to join the bishop in heaven. He went home, confessed, made his will, took the sacrament and quietly expired!

A
SUPERNATURAL LIGHT
A T
ST LEONARD'S PRIORY

THIS EVENT is told by Robert de Graystanes, the early fourteenth-century chronicler of Durham, elected bishop in 1333. Durham Abbey owned St. Leonard's Priory in Stamford.

On 12 March 1320, Sir Henry de Stanford, the former bishop of Durham, was buried in the choir of St. Leonard's Priory at Stamford. Suddenly before the altar a 'light shining from heaven, in the manner of a sunbeam' appeared, which was seen as a sign of divine approval of Stanford's opposition to Edward II and the Pope, who had deposed him from the bishopric of Durham. What is also remarkable is that Stanford was born on St. Leonard's day, was elected bishop of Durham on St. Leonard's day and was buried in St. Leonard's Priory.

A MIRACULOUS CURE

HIS mid seventeenth-century story is recorded in the second edition of Richard Butcher's *Survey of Stamford* of 1717 and is taken from a testimony written by Samuel Wallis, a Stamford shoemaker, upon whom the 'miracle' was performed.

Wallis was critically afflicted with consumption and William Foster, in a letter published in Peck's *Annals*, claimed that Wallis had been sick for thirteen years. On Whitsunday 1658 a stranger called at his house and begged for some small beer. He then instructed Wallis to take a herbal remedy of red sage leaves for twelve days after which time he would be cured. The miracle occurred just as predicted. Some people considered this stranger to be a devil changed into the illusion of an angel of light, or a witch. There was even a belief that he was the Wandering Jew, doomed to walk the earth until Christ's second coming. But the reality is probably less fantastic, as the prescribed remedy appears in the contemporary medicinal book, *Complete Herbal*, by Nicholas Culpeper.

A FRIAR'S PROPHECY

THE EARLIEST known reference to this tradition is in the *Stamford Mercury* of October 1825, at the time of Henry Fryer's bequests for the foundation of a hospital, and was copied by later writers.

According to a rhyme affixed to the gate, Walter de Heston predicted that:

Where once the white-robed friar with priestly state
Held his high rule within this hallowed gate,
Another ... fryer shall reign with healing skill,
And this blest site continue friar's still

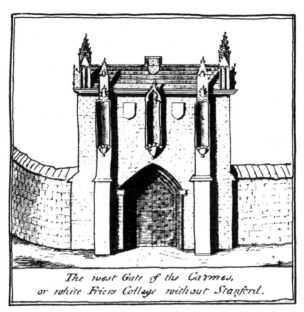

The west Gate of the Carmes,
or white Friers College without Stanford.

Greyfriars gate reproduced from Francis Peck's *Annals*, 1727.

The Stamford and Rutland Infirmary stands on the site of the Franciscan Greyfriars and was endowed by Henry Fryer, surgeon, in 1828.

The whole tale lacks credibility in that Heston, a noted academic who died *c.*1357, was not a Franciscan but a Carmelite of the Whitefriary, and his connection with Stamford is purely related to the university legend. The Whitefriars was until recently believed to stand on the hospital site, but it was actually positioned between St. Paul's Street and Priory Road. The surviving gateway to it is but a poor mutilated fragment, hardly a 'hallowed gate'. The tale is probably just a contemporary fabrication.

GHOST TALES

OR A town of such ancient importance, Stamford has remarkably few ghost traditions. There are no ghost references in any of the town's histories and Stamford does not appear in national ghost hunting books. Recently, the tourism business has invented a whole host of ghouls and apparitions, from phantom organists to the ghost of the bull-running, so that overnight Stamford became one of the most haunted towns in England. It will only be a matter of time before these enter the mythology of the town and join other oral traditions like the carriage in Star Lane or the Theatre ghost.

Besides Betty Clark's 'ghost story' in her *Stamford Remembered*, I have only found two recorded ghost tales about the town and both come from local newspapers. The first is in an article by Justin Simpson in the *Stamford Mercury* on Christmas Day 1891. It concerns a small field known as Emlyn's Close in the Northfields area of town:

Tradition says that a man named Emlyn, who owned the field, hanged himself from a tree opposite the Conduit head; and that in consequence it withered and never again bore leaves or showed any signs of life. In my younger days boys used to repeat these words:
Emlyn, Emlyn, let me go
Emlyn, Emlyn, bite my toe.
When thrice incanted after midnight the dead man would appear, seated on a white horse, and gallop round the field. That venerable authority 'the oldest inhabitant' has no recollection of ever seeing the spectre, nor has he heard of anybody who did see it. The legend as to the owner having thrown off this mortal coil in the manner indicated has not a tittle of truth.

So much for that tradition. The other incident was reported in the *Stamford and Rutland Guardian* on 26 March 1897:

The excitement of the week has centred round St. Mary's Place, where it is said there is a 'haunted' house. For a long time past, indeed ever since the tenant entered into possession (four years ago), strange, unpleasant and unaccountable noises have been heard in the house, generally between the hours of eleven at night and four in the morning, and so seriously has this state of things affected the tenant's family... that last Friday he moved his furniture to another house. Ever since then the house has been the centre of attraction, and in the evenings crowds have waited in the hope of seeing or hearing something of a ghostly nature. On Tuesday morning... a gentleman who is an unbeliever in ghosts... saw an apparition pass twice in front of the upstairs windows. He hastened to the house and on enquiry found that the only occupants were a servant girl and a washerwoman, and both were engaged downstairs. A search was immediately made of the house, but nothing was discovered.

From what we can gather, the noises which have been heard resemble a woman moaning and a man scolding, and on many occasions footsteps have been heard on the stairs repeatedly during the night, while the catches on the bedroom doors have been sounded and the doors opened. So great had the annoyance become that the servant girls could not be induced to go to bed, and the children manifested the greatest alarm and nervousness. On Friday night the whole of the upstairs windows were fastened, and we are informed by the gentleman who fastened them that, notwithstanding the fact that the house was tenantless and locked up, they were all wide open the following morning... We understand that two of the local clergy are anxious to pass a night in the house in order to get on speaking terms, if possible, with a visitor from the other world.

CUSTOMS

ESIDES THE main national customs and festivals such as Christmas, New Year and the agricultural seasonal festivals (Plough Monday, May Day and harvest festivals) which each region would adapt, many localities also evolved their own peculiar festivals and customs. Stamford had a particularly barbaric and unusual festivity - the bull-running - whose only parallel was at Tutbury in Staffordshire.

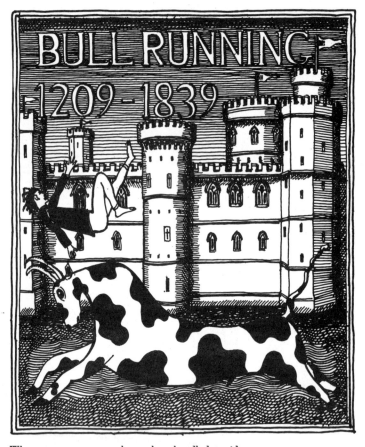

Where erst on conquest bent, though called to aid
The helpless Briton freed from Roman sway
And fearful of a second conqueror,
The fair-haired Saxon fought the barbarous Scot,
And then more equal matched the fairer Dane
In river pastures 'twixt their strongholds weak,
For centuries a mimic warfare waged
Such as arrested Warrenne's idle gaze
From out his Norman castle meadowwards,
Yet not so mimic but the baited bull
Endurance taught to generations who
Knew not to learn it from unsentient foes.
Rev. Claude Tickell, 'Bull Running', from *Guide to Old Stamford*, 1906.

THE
REBEL'S RIOT FEAST
THE TALE OF THE
STAMFORD
BULL RUNNING

...On this Day there is no King in Stamford; we are every one of us High
and Mighty. Lords of the united Parishes in a General Bull-running... we
are every one of us a Lord Paramount, a Lord of Rule and Misrule, a King
in Stamford... We are punishable for no Crime but Murder, and that only
of our own, and no other Species.
Francis Peck, *The Speech of a Notable Bullard about Forty Moons ago* from
his pamphlet of *c.*1723.

The bull-running custom was at one period the idol of the people of
Stamford; it was to them what the Olympic games were to the ancients of
Rome.
George Burton, *Chronology of Stamford,* 1846.

TAMFORD AND Tutbury in Staffordshire are
unique in England for their former indulgence in
the peculiar 'sport' of bull-running. Bull-baiting,
where a bull was tethered to a ring and goaded
by dogs and sticks, was relatively common, but
letting the bull roam through the streets was
nearer to Spanish than English custom.
(Pamplona in northern Spain still has
bull-running.) Peck in his satirical pamphlet on
bull-running says, 'I am sometimes inclined to believe the Stamfordians
and Spaniards are more closely related than most people imagine' and
Frederick Hackwood in an account of the Tutbury bull-running says it
might have originated 'in an imitation of Spanish bull-fighting,

introduced by John of Gaunt to please his wife Constance, a daughter of Pedro the Cruel of Castile'. But what of the Stamford custom?

The tradition, as related by Butcher, is that in 1209 (the date popularly associated with the introduction of bull-baiting into England), William de Warrenne, Lord of Stamford, on looking out from his castle walls, saw two bulls fighting for a cow in the castle meadows. Upon the intervention of a butcher and his mastiff dog, one of the bulls escaped into the town where it tossed men, women and children. The earl mounted his horse and chased after it, but enjoyed the sport so much that he ordered the town butchers to supply a mad bull every year on 13 November in return for grazing rights on the meadows. Whilst the tale itself is probably fictional, the butchers (known as 'triers') were often responsible for selecting the bull and the idea of a custom being supported by a charitable donation was common. The Tutbury bull was provided by the Duke of Devonshire and the famous Haxey Hood game in Lincolnshire probably arose from an earlier bull-running custom which involved the donation of a bull.

The actual origin of the Stamford custom is probably much older and the subject of much speculation. Mr. M. Holbeache Bloxam, a nineteenth-century archaeologist, believed the castle site was previously an ancient British earthwork - a memorial to the dead - around which a religious or social custom took place which evolved into bull-running. This· is obviously fantasy rather than fact. A Roman origin has been suggested, as bull-related sports were introduced into the empire by Julius Caesar, but there was no settlement at Stamford at that time. A Saxon origin is more plausible, for November was known as 'blood month', a month of sacrifice, and 13 November was St. Brice's Day - the anniversary of the massacre of the Danes by Ethelred II in 1002 (Stamford was the scene of Saxon and Danish conflict during the tenth century). Or possibly it was of Norman origin, for it is known from a twelfth-century description of London that bull-baiting was practised by them. They introduced the festival of Martinmas (11th November) and G. H. Burton alludes to the Irish custom of slaughtering an animal on St. Martin's Day, suggesting it was an earlier pagan practice brought into the Christian calendar. St. Brice and St. Martin were closely associated and St. Brice succeeded St. Martin as bishop of Tours in

444. St. Martin's church and its medieval guild were responsible at some stage for providing the bull. Peck says the St. Martin's guild was singled out in 1388 by Richard II as an example of the corruption within the guild system, because 'On the feast of St. Martin...the brethren have a certain bull.' He goes on to suggest that the 'mixture of bull-running, tipling and popery' was later used as a pretence by Edward VI to suppress the entire medieval guild system. The Tutbury bull-running was closely associated with the town's Court of Minstrels, established in the late fourteenth century, and took place on 15 August, the feast of the Assumption of the Virgin Mary. Mabel Peacock suggests (*Folklore* 15, 1944) that as Stamford lay at the junction of Rutland, Lincolnshire and Northamptonshire, perhaps 'the men of these shires anciently met by the Welland to observe the traditional rites intended to secure the prosperity of their territories'.

On the morning of 13 November the Stamford bellman would warn the townsfolk to shut up their doors, shops and gates and according to Richard Butcher

> which proclamation made, and the gates all shut up, the bull is turned out of the Alderman's [mayor's] house and then hivie, skivie, tag and rag, men, women and children of all sorts and sizes, with all the dogs in the town promiscuously run after him with their bull clubs, spattering dirt in each other's faces, that one would think them to be so many furies started out of hell...

Peck says

> The Streets are filled with Heroes who bandy the Dirt about their own Dublets, and take care that every Body who appears with a clean Face shall not want a dirty one; for He that gets no Bull-Dirt, gets no Christmas Pye.

Various means were employed to enrage the bull and G. H. Burton says: 'Hats were thrown at him, and frequently a hogshead [a large barrel] with the ends knocked out was brought, wherein a man placed himself, and, by rolling it to the bull, provoked him to toss it; but he tossed in vain, the occupant being too well trained to be easily dislodged.' Buckets of water were thrown in the bull's face and Harrod says that if a 'bad bull' was produced, the bullards were known to have

73

'sawn off his horns, cut off his tail, fired a train of gunpowder along his back, and poured aqua fortis (vitriol) on the same'. Peck adds that 'Some times they prod him with Needles, sometimes they pepper him, sometimes they Shoot at him.' The animal was 'pursued pell-mell by the multitude, through street after street, and sometimes across country, until, worn out by fatigue, and subdued by numbers, he was conducted back to his stable in triumph, men, women, and children clinging to his horns, head, tail and every part to "load" him' (Samuel Sharp). The bull driven to exhaustion, would then be baited (at the bull ring near Lammas Bridge on Bath Row) or killed straight away, whence:

> The body is shared by the Heroes, and in old time, he who first rode upon the Bull's Back, had the head... [and] The Great Gut, or pudding, commonly known by the name of Tom Hodge, be given to the most Worthy Adventurer.
> **Francis Peck**

In later years the main object was to topple the bull from the town bridge whereupon it would be killed and roasted for a huge supper of 'bull-beef'. If the animal proved to be a 'beast of spirit' and could not be 'brigged' its life was spared, but if it was a 'bad bull' and could be 'brigged' by midday then the bullards held themselves entitled to another bull at Christmas. In the Tutbury custom the bull had his horns, ears and tail cut off, his body smeared with soap and his nose blown full of pepper. The minstrels and people of the town ran after the bull and the person who could cut off a piece of its skin before it crossed into Derbyshire was declared the owner and King of the Music's Bull. The bull was then baited as the Stamford one occasionally was. If the bull passed into Derbyshire it remained the property of the donor. Harrod is dismissive of the Tutbury custom and quotes a verse:

> Tutbury's to Stamford's - Gods! what a sound!
> A penny to a thousand pound,
> A cock-boat to a man of war,
> A meteor to a blazing star.

Strange customs arose around the Stamford 'sport'. The bullards, or bull chasers, would secretly prepare uncouth and wild costumes and the week before the chase their imps would holler through the town, 'Hoy, bull, hoy!', in anticipation of the excitement. Peck states, 'the bullards make their Appearance, habited Ten Thousand Times more nastily than so many Witches on a Plow Monday'. According to Burton rough watercolour drawings of bull-running incidents, known as 'bull-for-evers', were sold on the festal day and were often mounted on the bullard's hat. Peck adds that the private or 'stop' bull-runnings, which became popular in later years, had an effigy of St. Andrew, who replaced Taurus in the Christian 'Apostolic Zodiac'. This device was suspended by rope from the upper windows of the houses and as the bull charged, it would be hoisted into the air leaving 'Old Roger' to career futilely forward. At the 1836 festival a disguised police officer saw '...two men, with an effigy of a man stuffed and coloured red, holding it in front of the bull. The bull tossed the effigy out of their hands and became very infuriated.' Additionally, hogsheads were placed at various points, around which the bullards could manoeuvre and George Burton claims that 'It is notorious that the Stamford Bullards were amongst the most courageous men to be found in the country.'

In later years a 'bull queen', or 'bull woman', dressed all in blue and carrying a blue bull stick, would preside over the day's activities and she would be responsible for raising money to provide the bull. Brian Jewell in *Fairs and Revels* suggests that the queen was originally a man dressed as a woman, but George Burton believed the tradition began in 1789 during an attempted suppression of the 'sport'. In that year the bull was brought into the town through St. George's Gate by Ann Blades, to the astonishment of the assembled constables and Second Dragoon guards. The bullards appearing peaceable, the officer told his men to dismiss, at which point the bull was let loose and the troops joined in! Ann Blades held the office of 'Empress of the Bullards' or 'Nan Roberts', as she was alternatively called, until her death in 1808, when she was succeeded by Mrs Jorden. The tradition ended in 1828 when the bull woman apparently burnt her clothes of office and joined the Methodist church. A bull woman was depicted in the famous early nineteenth-century bull-running painting of a scene in Broad Street. She also featured in a carving on a 'bull pitcher' made from the

75

The Stamford bull-running based on the original painting by Mr. Everard, *c.*1800, (now lost).

horn of the bull run in 1799, which shows her wearing a crown and holding a flag with the words, 'God save the king and a bull for ever'.

Numerous bull songs were written and 'at the public-houses and at other convivial assemblies in the town for six weeks before and six weeks after the Taurine festival it was customary for men to sing the glories of the sport' (G. H. Burton). The most famous was composed, according to J. Clare Billing, by four natives of the town and set to the tune of a Scottish dance which was performed by the town waits. G. H. Burton considered this was reminiscent of Coleridge's political satire, *Recantation, Illustrated by the Story of the Mad Ox*, written in the early nineteenth century. The music was printed in Burton's articles:

SONG OF THE STAMFORD BULLARDS.

Words and Music Anonymous.

Arranged for Piano by ALLAN RIPPON.

Come, all you bon-ny boys Who love to bait the bon-ny bull, Who take de-light in noise, And you shall have your bel-ly-full. On Stamford's Town Bull run-ning day, We'll show you such right gal-lant play, You nev-er saw the like, you'll say, As you have seen at Stamford.

2. Earl Warenne was the man
That first began this gallant sport;
In the Castle he did stand,
And saw the bonny bulls that fought;
The butchers with their bull-dogs came,
These sturdy stubborn bulls to tame,
But more with madness did inflame,
Enrag'd they ran through Stamford.

3. Delighted with the Sport,
The meadows there he freely gave,
Where these bonny bulls had fought,
The butchers now do hold and have:
By charter they are strictly bound,
That every year a bull be found:
Come daub your face you dirty clown,
And stump away to Stamford.

4. Come, take him by the tail boys,-
Bridge, bridge him if you can;
Prog him with a nail boys;
Never let him quiet stand;
Through every street and lane in town
We'll chevy chase him up and down;
You sturdy strawyards ten miles round,
Come stump away to Stamford.

5. Bring with you a prog stick, -
Boldly mount then on his back.
Bring with you a dog Dick,
Who will also help to bark.
This is the rebel's riot feast,
Humanity must be debas'd
And every man must do his best
To bait the bull in Stamford.

Another bull tale concerns the famous early nineteenth-century actor, Mr. Macready, who was assailed after a fine performance of Hamlet at Stamford Theatre, with the dual cry of 'Macready', on the one hand, and 'bull' from a confused section on the other - in request of the bull song. Macready was incensed by this and demanded to know its

78

meaning. On hearing of the bull-running tradition he was disgusted and replied in best Shakespearean verse:

I presume your dull ass will not mend his face with beating but this
Stamford custom 'All sense doth eat of habit's devil
Imperious Caesar, dead and turned to clay.
Might stop a hole to keep the wind away;
O for Jove's thunder to stem this foolish roar -
A Stamford "Bull" in truth is but a boor [bore].

During the eighteenth century the sport increasingly became a recreation of the working classes. 'Stop' bull-runnings became popular and were held on single streets blocked by carts, often on the initiation of the publicans. St. Leonard's Street, Sheepmarket and Broad Street were notorious arenas for these events which could occur at any time through the winter months. Peck quotes a tradition that these bull runnings began in the reign of Queen Mary 'in imitation of the Protestants who were hem'd in with Faggots and burnt to Death'.

But attitudes to popular custom were changing. The growth of industrialisation and Nonconformism resulted in the collapse of the old traditionally supported customs and public charities. These were replaced with a new paternalism based on moral and physical 'improvement', where the poor were distanced. W. E. H. Lecky in his *History of the Rise and Influence of the Spirit of Rationalism in Europe* said 'Amusements that were once universal passed from the women to the men, from the upper to the lower classes, from the virtuous to the vicious, until at last the Legislature interposed to suppress them.' Thus the church, the corporation, and the gentry began to divorce themselves from the bull-running. As early as 1741, St. George's Church stopped its traditional bull-subscriptions and Harrod writing in 1785 commented that 'the Chief Magistrate will not suffer him [the bull] to set a foot in his barn, nor his stable, nor anything that is his'. In 1778 the Tutbury bull-running was suppressed and the gentry of Stamford seeing the cruelty and barbarity of their festival were prompted into action. In a 'stop run' organised by the landlord of the Half Moon on St. Paul's Street during Christmas 1776, the *Mercury* reported that 'several people were toss'd, and one man, terribly bruis'd and gor'd in the face, by

79

which it is fear'd he will lose one of his eyes' and in 1785 the underbutler of Burghley House was killed when the bull suddenly turned on him. On 31 October 1788 an advertisment produced by the Corporation and supported by the Earl of Exeter appeared in the *Stamford Mercury*. It claimed that bull-running was

> a custom of such unparalleled cruelty to an innocent animal, and in all respects a disgrace to religion, law and nature

and warned that

> And whereas some evilminded, loose, idle and disorderly persons think proper to threaten the Magistracy and inhabitants of this Borough... such threatened meeting will be unlawful and punishable by DEATH...

A published sermon on bull-running preached by J. F. Winks in 1829 claimed the custom 'resembled more a scene amongst the savages of New Zealand than amongst the inhabitants of a respectable town in England'. and he added that 'I never beheld more bold, daring, unblushing, unbridled vice and licentiousness in open day.' Drakard, though, in his *Stamford News* of 17 November 1819 accused the sport's antagonisers of hypocrisy, as many of them were fox hunters, suggesting their real motive was purely to destroy a working class tradition:

> Away, then, with this spurious feeling and bastard humanity! which froths and foams at one yearly indulgence of the lower orders, and sympathises with the daily and destructive enjoyments of the high and the wealthy...

But, as elsewhere, the old customs were resilient. The attempted suppression of 1788-89 involved troops and police but was ineffectual and only incited new fervour. Many pro-bull pamphlets and song sheets were produced, and one of *c*.1800 proclaimed:

> A Bull, depend upon it, there will always be while a certain female lives [probably Ann Blades], or while one stone stands upon another in Stamford. Shall it be said in after ages, that we have been cowards, and given up what our ancestors have been so much delighted with, and even we have tasted the pleasure so often? No our children shall not say we are

80

afraid, but we'll set them an example to keep it up, and be true Stamfordians.

Additional miniature bull-runnings, sponsored by public houses, were common in the early nineteenth century and the organisation of the festival transferred to the poorer areas of the town. St. Leonard's Street became the centre of operations; the Olive Branch Inn (no. 3, in existence c.1826-1959) was the bullards' headquarters and the Royal Oak (no. 60, in existence c.1796-1906) provided stabling for the bull. The importance of the custom was such that parliamentary candidates in the contested elections of 1809 and 1812 bribed the poorer electorate with the promise of a bull. As late as 1831, the Tory, or Burghley, candidate canvassed under the large flag of a painted bull, despite the Marquess of Exeter's opposition to the custom. It was ironic, though, that without the official opposition the bull-running would probably have faded quietly away into obscurity. Real interest in the tradition was actually waning; during the 1820s great difficulty was experienced in procuring money for a bull and the last Christmas run occurred in 1831.

Interest was revived in 1833 when a Mr. Wheeler from the Society for the Prevention of Cruelty to Animals, supported by various Nonconformists, arrived at Stamford in a new campaign to suppress the 'sport'. He was roughly handled by the mob and forcibly removed from the town. By 1836 five to six thousand people packed into St. Leonard's Street for a 'stop run'. The Society's efforts to prosecute the ringleaders at the Lincoln Assizes in 1837 further increased the mob's passion. G. H. Burton says

In spite of humane and eloquent appeals in the local newspapers and magazines; convictions at assizes; fines by the local magistrates; motions in the Queen's Bench; mandates from Lord John Russell; detachments of metropolitan police; and the presence of cavalry with carbines loaded with ball cartridge - in spite of all these obstacles the sport was carried on for several years.

In 1838 a troop of Nottinghamshire dragoons and the metropolitan police were attacked with stones and bricks and in 1839 the government brought in the 5th Dragoon guards to suppress the bull running once and for all. Despite their presence a bull was still run through the streets, to the enjoyment of some four thousand people, and the burden of the cost (around £300) was born by Stamford. This expense roused many residents from their apathy, and following negotiations with the bullards, the town itself succeeded in preventing the custom which appears to have died away with little opposition - an indication of the actual decline in real interest. The middle decades of the nineteenth century saw the suppression of similar large set-piece festivals, including the Tutbury bull-running which had continued illegally until 1840. The memory lingered on, though, in the minds of many Stamford people. Bull suppers were common and the Bull Song was a popular request right up until the end of the nineteenth century. It even persisted into the twentieth century and the Infirmary produced a *Bullard's Rag Mag* during the 1950s.

Of the bull-running objects that still survive, the most important are the two paintings which hang, rather ironically, in the Mayor's Office in Stamford Town Hall. The main painting shows a scene in Broad Street outside Browne's Hospital and is the 'third' bull-running painting referred to by G. H. Burton in his *Old Lincolnshire* articles. It appears to be a copy of what Burton called 'the oldest and best' of the paintings, which is a smaller work of c.1800 (24 by 18 inches) and was painted by a Mr. Everard who was buried in St. George's Church around 1835. This painting is now lost but a photograph of it was reproduced in *Stamford Then and Now*, a limited edition commemorative volume produced by Stamford Corporation in 1951, and the drawing on page 76 is a copy of it. The figures are better grouped on this version and the bull-woman is more in proportion. The other bull-running painting is the work of James Smeeton who died in 1883 and shows the 1839 bull being escorted by troops into Scotgate after its escape to Tolethorpe.

PLOUGH MONDAY

Twelfth Day doth cooks and butlers glad,
Whilst losing cards makes gamesters mad;
Plow-day brings witches and much noise,
Whilst bloody *Tuesday* frights schoolboys.
Poor Robin's Almanack, 1741, reproduced in **Brand's** *Popular Antiquities.*

F THE more common festivals the most interesting of those mentioned in the *Stamford Mercury* is Plough Monday, which is reported during the mid-nineteenth century. Plough Monday was originally a festival to ensure the ease of ploughing and the propagation of the seed. It took place on the Monday after Twelfth Day when the farm workers returned to work after the Christmas holiday. In 1874 the *Mercury* reported that the custom was in decline but 'formerly several gangs of "plough-witches", ludicrously dressed and with hideous painted faces, came in from the country and visited the tradesmen's shops, levying "black-mail" and generally terminating their begging rounds with drunken orgies'. In 1862 the *Mercury* was appalled that one drunken excess had continued at a public house until seven in the morning! This seems to have been the extent of the later celebrations, for in 1862 the *Mercury* reported that no plough was drawn through the streets as was common in the festival. The term 'plough-witches' is local to this area but it is also recorded in Huntingdonshire. Peck in his bull-running pamphlet of 1723 insults the bullards by saying they were 'habited Ten Thousand Times more nastily than so many Witches on a Plow Monday'. They were more commonly called plough-bullocks from the fact that they pulled the plough in the procession. The plough-witches often wore women's clothing, which was derived from the mummers' plays where an old woman called Bessy, accompanied by the fool, was the central character who carried the money box. In 1864 the *Mercury* complained about the 'country louts who disfigured themselves by daubing their faces with red and black paint, and by wearing bonnets, gowns and

shawls...' An unusual version of the Plough Monday custom has recently been revived at Whittlesea, near Peterborough, where a straw bear is the main feature of the procession.

THE
STAMFORD WAITS
& BELLMAN

In mode of olden time
His garb was fashion'd, to express
The ancient English minstrel's dress,
A seemly gown...
It seem'd some masquer's quaint array,
For revel or for holiday
Sir Walter Scott, *Rokeby*, canto XV.

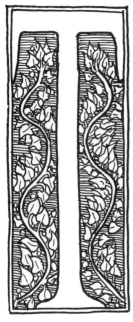

HE WAITS were a group of four musicians or minstrels who performed for the local corporation and received a badge and annual payment for their services. They represented a common English custom dating back to the Middle Ages and were first mentioned in Stamford in 1486. Their best description is from Harrod in 1785:

> The waits have an annual salary of fifty shillings each, these drest in scarlet cloaks trimmed with gold lace precede the Mayor with their music the day he is chosen, commonly called the Mayor's feast day; on proclaiming of the Simon and Jude fair [in November] and on his Majesty's birthday; thrice weekly also in the dead of night they walk round the streets playing from the above fair until Christmas, at which holidays they call at persons' houses where after playing a tune or two they are presented with a shilling or half-a-crown at the donor's pleasure.

The waits performed the bull tune in the period surrounding the bull festival and were closely associated with the bellman, who would walk around the town between midnight and two in the morning on the days when the waits were not playing. Justin Simpson, in his article on the Stamford waits in *The Reliquary* in July 1885, describes them crying out in the night after the performance of a tune these words by Shakespeare;

Deep night, dark night, the silent of the night,
The time of night when Troy was set on fire;
The time when scritch-owls cry, and ban-dogs howl,
And spirits walk and ghosts break up their graves.

The waits were officially disbanded in 1832 but existed as an independent body until the late nineteenth century, by which time their peculiar custom was becoming more than a little irritating to certain residents of the town. In November 1894, Carew H. St. John Mildmay, the Anglo-Catholic rector of St. Mary's church, wrote in a letter to the *Mercury*:

I regard the prospect of their movements at two o'clock on Sunday mornings, with absolute dread. The whole thing is to me like a bad dream. And they are so merciless: they go on and on: they seem untiring. It is as if they had drawn off into themselves almost all the energy of Stamford.

Fortunately for Mr. Mildmay, the tradition died out shortly afterwards. Six waits' badges still survive at the Town Hall, four bear the date 1691 and the other two, 1823.

Stamford bellman based on early drawing reproduced in Roger's *Book of Stamford*.

KISSING THE OLD MAN AT STAMFORD SCHOOL

It is my intent,
And on it I'm bent,
In our Spacious Hall,
The School Roll to Call,
Of those who have felt
From foot to the belt
Most cruelly pinched
And woefully lynched,
While kissing the face -
With horrid grimace
And very poor grace -
Of the School Old Man.
Anonymous poem published in *The Stamfordian*, Lent Term, 1887.

THE CUSTOM of kissing the Old Man at Stamford School is of unknown origin, but it was an established tradition by Victorian times. It was a type of initiation ceremony for new boys and took place during Saturday break when two prefects held each new boy up in turn to kiss the Old Man to the accompaniment of the ironical applause of the whole school. The Old Man was a medieval carved head which formed the keystone of the door into the old school, formerly St. Paul's Church. In 1929 the worn head was reset into the west door of the chapel extension and this was the foundation stone laid by Lord Burghley. B. L. Deed in *A History of Stamford School* quotes two nineteenth-century references to the custom. Arthur Browning, the son of Stamford architect Edward Browning, who was at the school in the 1870's, reports that 'The initiation of the new boys kissing the face of the "Old Man", which forms the keystone of the church door, was seldom practised' and J. H. Boam of the same period recalled that the ceremony was only undertaken if a pupil had done anything to dishonour the school. The tradition was suppressed by the school in 1961.

PEOPLE

EOPLE ALSO become the subject of legend. Sometimes their life stories are so unusual that truth is stranger than fiction. Others are famous or notorious people who generate so many tales that it is hard to separate what is true and what is not. Either way their lives are outstanding enough to capture the popular imagination; they are remembered and they become part of the town's history. Often their connection with the place is very slight or even non-existent. Dick Turpin is claimed to have stopped here and according to Nevinson, Queen Elizabeth dined at the Whitefriars in 1565, after which it fell to the ground. This chapter introduces a few of Stamford's more interesting people and includes murderers, political idealists, oddities of nature and romantic aristocrats.

ROMANCE

HENRY CECIL

AND THE

COTTAGE COUNTESS

THE MARRIAGES of Henry Cecil, the first Marquess of Exeter, have attracted considerable popular interest. In 1842 Alfred Tennyson wrote a romantic and fanciful ballad based on Cecil, entitled *The Lord of Burleigh*. Tennyson's inaccurate account, in which Cecil marries a lowly 'village maiden' who subsequently dies very young under 'the burden of an honour unto which she was not born', was later accepted as truth by later writers on the subject. The real events, though, are just as fascinating.

Henry Cecil was born in 1754 in Brussels. He was the son of a black sheep of the family, Thomas Chambers Cecil by his French wife, Charlotte Gormier. After nine months, Henry was adopted by Thomas' older brother, the ninth Earl, whose own marriage was childless. Henry became successor to the Burghley estate and in return the ninth Earl settled his younger brother's debts. In 1776, Henry married Emma Vernon, who had inherited a wealthy estate at Hanbury in Worcestershire. In the style of his father he squandered the Vernon fortune and he alienated his wife. After thirteen years of childless marriage, Emma Cecil ran away with the Rev. William Sneyd, the curate of Hanbury. They eloped to Exeter and after the divorce, they married and lived in Portugal where Sneyd died in 1793.

In the court case of June 1790, Henry Cecil was awarded £1000 damages and a divorce, but what makes the whole story so remarkable is that by this time he was already secretly remarried. After his wife's departure in 1789, Henry retired to the village of Bolas Magna in Shropshire to escape both the scandal and his heavy gambling debts. He changed his name to John Jones and fell in love with a seventeen-year-old village girl called Sarah Hoggins. He married her under his false name in Bolas Magna church in April 1790 and he built a large house there for them both. After the divorce he married her again under his real name at St. Mildred's, Bread Street, London and their first child, Sophia, was born in July 1792. Little is known of the 'cottage countess' but there is no evidence of her surprise at seeing Burghley House, or her supposed decline under the aristocratic social pressures which Tennyson alludes to. She died in 1797, aged 23, after giving birth to their fourth child.

After marrying one woman from the landed gentry and another from the people, Cecil's third marriage was from the high ranks of the peerage. In August 1800 he married Elizabeth Burrell, whose marriage to Douglas, the 6th Duke of Hamilton, was dissolved in 1799. Henry continued to live a life of excess. He built numerous estate buildings, including the Bottle Lodges which cost around £9,000, and was constantly in debt. He became the first Marquess of Exeter in 1801 and he died in 1804, aged 50.

CRIME

THOMAS FULLER BACON
THE
'WALWORTH MURDERER'

In Stamford Town he once did dwell,
In deeds of darkness none could him excel;
Not all the world, your life can save,
They know the secrets of thy Parents' graves.
Anonymous poem from contemporary London pamphlet.

IN THE late 1850s Stamford was the centre of an extraordinary murder case which filled the national and international press. Indeed, such was its notoriety that London broadsheets and poems were issued describing

89

and exaggerating the incident. Yet there was never any definite proof that Bacon was guilty of the crimes with which he was charged. This account is taken from reports in the *Stamford Mercury* during 1857.

Thomas Fuller Bacon was born in Stamford in 1824 and was considered to be stubborn, selfish and unsociable as a child. He followed his father's profession as a whitesmith, locksmith, bell hanger and general ironmonger and lived in a house in Broad Street where he fiddled the local gas company by bypassing the meter using a section of old piping. He then seduced the daughter of a respectable tradesman and is supposed to have deserted her after getting her pregnant. He later married her and after his father's death he was able to buy a house in St. Peter's Hill. At his father's funeral he is rumoured to have said "There is now only the old woman's death to pray for" (he stood to inherit property in the town worth £900).

Bacon, however, soon came into financial difficulties and he tried to foil a £90 debt owed to a local stonemason by forging a receipt. On discovery of the fraud, though, he destroyed the receipt to avoid incrimination. One night during 1856 his house was burnt to the ground and he was tried before Lincoln Assizes on a charge of arson of which he was acquitted.

Around November 1856, Bacon and his family moved to Walworth in London and on 29 December their two children, Edwin Fuller Bacon, aged 2½, and Sarah Ann Bacon, aged 11 months, were brutally murdered by having their throats cut. As Thomas was apparently away in Reigate, Martha, his wife, aged 26, who had a history of mental illness, was charged with the murder. She pleaded that she did not do it and her husband's inconsistencies and contradictions aroused suspicion. Martha then blamed her husband for the act and this revived interest in the sudden death of Bacon's mother, Ann, at Stamford in May 1855.

She had fallen ill following a dinner at her son's house and had shown symptoms of arsenic poisoning. It was further established that Bacon had purchased some arsenic from a shop in Red Lion Square only days before, allegedly to kill rats. The cause of death at the time was diagnosed as 'cerebral disease' and there was no inquiry. *The Times* later stated:

The public will learn with surprise that a circumstance so pregnant with suspicion should have been allowed to occur in so populous a town as Stamford without a proper judicial inquiry.

The exhumation of the body, which was buried at Great Casterton church, was ordered, but the Stamford and Rutland officials refused to co-operate, probably out of embarrassment if a different judgement were to be found. Eventually the Home Office intervened and in February 1857 a post mortem was held and a verdict of wilful murder recorded. In May, Thomas and Martha were tried in London for the murder of their children; Thomas was found not guilty - as there was no evidence to suggest a motive, or that he was in the area at the time - and Martha was acquitted on the grounds of insanity.

Thomas Bacon was then brought to Stamford to face the charge of poisoning his mother and was committed to Lincoln for trial. Despite a statement by Martha that she poisoned Ann Bacon, Thomas was found guilty, but as there was no absolute proof he was sentenced to imprisonment for life. The sentence disappointed many people whose prejudice had wanted him hanged, including those pamphleteers who had established his guilt long before any trial.

JOHN GEORGE HAIGH
THE
ACID BATH MURDERER

JOHN GEORGE HAIGH was executed on 10 August 1949 for the murder, in London, of Olive Durand-Deacon, a wealthy widow. What made the whole case so remarkable was his confession to five other murders, his bizarre method of removing the evidence - by dissolving the bodies in acid - and his claims that he indulged in vampirism. He claimed he associated himself with an abnormality that characterised the outstanding personalities of history, such as Confucius, Jesus Christ, Julius Caesar and Hitler. He was always immaculately presented, exuding self-confidence and charm, and appeared totally detached from the horrific nature of his crimes, which he believed were a 'mission' he had to perform.

Haigh was born in Stamford at no. 22 King's Road on 24 July 1909, the son of an engineer. His parents were members of the fundamentalist Plymouth Brethren and their strict religion dominated his early life. The family left Stamford some time before 1916 and most of his childhood was spent in Yorkshire near Outwood Colliery. Haigh returned to Stamford on a number of occasions and during the 1940s he often stayed at the George Hotel.

CASSANDRA KING
STAMFORD'S LAST EXECUTION

CASSANDRA KING was the last person to be condemned to death in Stamford and because of this her story has become exaggerated. She was found guilty of a burglary at Wothorpe in 1704, but there is a story that after her execution proof of her innocence was found and that this was the reason for stopping capital punishment at Stamford. According to the Rev. William Forster, who visited her in jail, she had prayed that the weather on the day of her execution should be fine. Miraculously the unsettled weather at the time cleared and the day was sunny!

The gallows were situated on the 'Lings' near the road to Little Casterton (on the site of the brickworks). She was buried in St. Michael's Churchyard in the north-east corner.

POLITICS

ROBERT OWEN
UTOPIAN REFORMER

OBERT OWEN was the most experimental industrialist of his time and his humanitarian and philosophical ideas had a profound effect upon later generations.

He was born in Wales in 1771 but served his apprenticeship in Stamford at the drapery business of James McGuffog, where he stayed for three years, originally at 31 High Street and later on St. Mary's Street. Burghley Park became his study and there he formulated his religious ideas which were to alienate him from society for the rest of his life. He considered that all the world's religions had originated from a single source and were the 'imaginations formed when such men were ignorant of their own nature, were devoid of experience, and were governed by their random conjectures which... were far from the truth'. He replaced his religious feelings with a spirit of universal charity of which the fundamental basis was the belief that character is formed by experience and circumstances (John Locke had originated this theory in the seventeenth century). It was therefore important that a benevolent society should mould people to goodness and there should be no expression of negative emotion such as anger and punishment.

Owen devoted the rest of his life in putting these principles into practice. His mills at New Lanark were supported by a system of liberal education and an Institute for the Formation of Character. He later helped establish a utopian community called New Harmony in America and even became converted to spiritualism, writing some posthumous dramas by Shakespeare.

Robert Owen is still influential today and a newly-restored New Lanark is now a shrine for Japanese businessmen eager to explore his system of benign authoritarian socialism.

ARNOLD SPENCER LEESE
ANTI-SEMITIC CAMEL VET

RNOLD LEESE was the most extreme anti-Semitic figure in British Fascist politics during the 1930s, and his views were closer to those of the German National Socialists than any other political leader. He came to Stamford after the First World War and lived in the town during the 1920s at no. 20 St. George's Square. Leese was a vet by trade, but no ordinary vet, for he was a specialist in camels, having spent twenty years in India and Africa studying their diseases. He wrote a standard text book on the subject which was published in Stamford by Haynes and Son. He was a non-smoker, a teetotaller and a lover of animals, but what really preoccupied him was an overwhelming and violent anti-Semitism, derived perhaps from his dislike of the kosher method of slaughtering animals.

This hatred and distrust was fuelled when Arthur Kitson of Kitson Empire Lighting Company in Stamford introduced him to the famous anti-Semitic forgery *The Protocols of the Elders of Zion*, which claimed that the Jews were about to take over the world (an example of modern mythologising for political purposes). He even suspected Christianity of being part of a Jewish plot to undermine the virility of the Nordic races.

In 1924, Leese joined the British Fascists, but more as an anti-socialist and anti-semite, and his Stamford group soon broke away from the mainstream Fascist movement. Leese later claimed that the Stamford Fascists were the first to adopt the black shirt - later to become the uniform of Mosley's movement in the 1930s. Another first for Leese was that Stamford was the only place in the country where Fascists fought and won an election, for in contesting an election Leese

broke the cardinal rule of the British Fascists never to intervene in the despised democratic system. In 1924, two Labour candidates stood unopposed in the Stamford municipal election and this prompted Leese and fellow Fascist Henry L. Simpson, an engineer, to stand against them. Amazingly, they won, and Simpson was re-elected in 1927 despite both Conservative and Labour opposition.

Leese, however, was unhappy with Stamford, realising it was a 'poor base from which to run a national revolution', and in 1927 he moved to Guildford where he formed the Imperial Fascist League. Their racialist Fascist policies and activities were a thorn in the flesh of Sir Oswald Mosley's movement throughout the 1930s, and their flag was the Union Jack with a swastika in the centre.

After the outbreak of the Second World War Leese went into hiding, but was arrested and imprisoned in November 1940. He was only apprehended after giving one of the detectives searching his home a hefty kick up the backside! He then smashed up his cell and began his detention with a three month sentence for assault and wilful damage. Hitler's defeat in 1945 did little to deter Leese and he continued his anti-Jewish activities until his death in 1956. In 1960 the headquarters of the new British National Party was given the title of Arnold Leese House.

NATURAL ODDITIES

DANIEL LAMBERT
& TOM THUMB

DANIEL LAMBERT, the 'extraordinary and celebrated human mammoth', died in Stamford in 1809 aged 39. At the time of his death he was the heaviest man in Britain, weighing almost 53 stone (336kg) and measuring 3ft 11in around the leg and 9ft 4in around the waist. The heaviest recorded man in Britain is now Peter Yarnell of East Ham, London, who weighed 59 stone and died in 1984, aged 34.

Daniel Lambert based on a painting by Benjamin Marshall (1768-1835).

Lambert was born in Leicester in 1770 and succeeded his father as keeper of Bridewell Prison. His weight increased rapidly from an early age - the result of a natural physical disorder, not over-indulgence - and at the age of 23 he weighed 32 stone. After the closure of the prison in 1805, Lambert reluctantly decided to exhibit himself in London, and travelled there in a specially constructed coach. He received a wide variety of curious people eager to see his immense bulk, including the famous Polish dwarf Count Barulawski - their meeting being compared to the fable of the people of Lilliput and Brobdingnag from Swift's *Gulliver's Travels*. A description of him written in 1806 states:

> When seated, his thighs are so covered by his belly, that nothing but his knees are to be seen; while the flesh on his legs, which represents stuffed pillows, projects in such a manner as nearly to bury his feet!

Numerous tales appeared, the most illustrious being the incident when Lambert fearlessly struck Bruin, a performing bear which had attacked his dog. The bear apparently fled in terror, yelling and howling, but contemporary accounts tell a different story, where the bear in fact knocked Lambert down and he was so fat he could not get up!

Lambert came to Stamford to exhibit himself during the horse races which took place on Wittering Heath to the south of the town. He lodged at the Waggon and Horses Inn, no. 47-50, High Street St. Martin's, and died suddenly on the morning of 21 June 1809. A window and a section of wall had to be removed to take out the body and twenty men were needed to lower the coffin into his grave in St. Martin's Churchyard, where his tombstone states 'in personal greatness [he] had no competitor'. A national newspaper at the time exclaimed:

> Nature had endured all the trespass she could admit; the poor man's corpulancy had constantly increased until at the time we have mentioned the clogged machinery of life stood still and this prodigy of mammon was numbered with the dead.

His only surviving set of clothes was exhibited for many years at the London Inn on St. John's Street, and the American dwarf Charles Stratton ('General Tom Thumb') visited Stamford in 1846, 1859, and with his wife Livinia Warren and Commodore Nutt and Minnie Warren in 1866, to view the phenomenon. An armhole of the waistcoat went round all four of them! 'Tom Thumb' left a set of his own clothes as a comparison and both are now on display in Stamford Museum.

ANTIQUARIANISM

WILLIAM STUKELEY
THE ARCH DRUID

HEN William Stukeley arrived in Stamford in 1729 to take up the living of All Saints' Church, he was already a well-known physician and public figure, and today he is still remembered as one of the father figures of British archaeology. In 1718 he had helped to form the Society of Antiquaries in London and he had already begun his revolutionary survey work into the Stonehenge and Avebury stone circles. On his arrival Francis Peck, a fellow antiquarian, showered him with romantic and mythical titles which pleased Stukeley greatly:

> Warden of the Augustin Fryers, Capellan of Bredecroft Chapel and St. Mary's Chantry, President of the Black Hall, Peterborough Hall, Sempringham Hall, Durham and Vaudy.

Stukeley first took up residence in St. Peter's Rectory and later in a large house at the top of Barn Hill. Here he began writing his *Mosaic Chronology* - a book in three parts on Patriarchal Christianity of which only the Stonehenge and Avebury sections were published. This was the

Drawing based on Stukeley's plan of his house and garden, with a plan of
Stonehenge superimposed over it. Druid figure and Temple of Flora at Stamford
also derived from Stukeley's own drawings.

first systematic survey of stone circles ever to be undertaken and in it Stukeley attempted to prove that the Druids, whom he believed built the circles, were the forefathers of Christianity. He believed the Druids had come to England as part of an 'oriental colony' of Phoenicians of Abraham's religion, whose leader was the Tyrian Hercules. Through a bizarre collection of Biblical and Classical allusions, these Druids, worshipping in their 'serpent' or 'dragon' temples in expectation of the Messiah, became the ancestors of the Church of England. This theory was to be one of the central beliefs of Stukeley's historical and religious philosophy.

He began a friendship with William Warburton, the famous clerical controversialist and vicar of Brant Broughton near Newark, and Stukeley's history of Stamford is in the form of an elaborate and flowery dialogue between 'Palaephatus' (Stukeley) and 'Panagius' (Warburton). In it Stukeley happily explores the early mythology of the town. In 1736 he began a series of strange publications which further examined the supposed links between Biblical and Classical characters, including *A Comment on an Ode of Horace, Showing the Bacchus of the Heathen to be the Jehovah of the Jews.* Also in that year he formed the Stamford Brazenose Society and at their first meeting they discussed astronomy and the latitude of Stamford, lunar maps, a remarkable wasps' nest and a 'stone as big as a walnut, taken from out of the bladder of a little Dutch dog'.

Stukeley also began enthusiastically landscaping the garden of his house in Barn Hill and devised a formal garden on a concentric circular layout which could have been based on his Stonehenge plan (see drawing). He also built a picturesque hermitage of a 'Very Gothique and rude Nature' and a 'theatrical' Temple of Flora with medieval stained glass windows salvaged from Stamford's churches.

By the 1740s, Stukeley's beliefs were becoming more obscure. He became preoccupied by the mysteries of the book of Revelation, King Solomon's Temple (he was a freemason), and Isis from Egyptian religion. He also became friends with the eccentric Duke of Montagu of Boughton House in Northamptonshire, for 'In Stamford... there was not one person, clergy or lay, that had any taste of learning or ingenuity, so that I was actually as much dead in converse as in a coffin.' The Duke

The Hermitage in Stukeley's Barn Hill garden, drawn by Stukeley, 1738.

had a passion for practical jokes - wetting people with hoses and putting itching powder in their beds - and he was a devoted animal lover, always surrounded by dogs and preferring the ugliest because no-one else would be kind to it. Stukeley had a strong affection for his cat 'Tit', describing her as 'an uncommon creature and of all I ever know the most sensible, most loving'.

In 1747, Stukeley could stand Stamford no longer and he took up the living of St. George's in Bloomsbury, London, thus ending his associations with the town. In his notebooks, which are now in the British Library, he lamented:

> and thus ended the last of my dull years in the country, without any hope, or desire of a removal. I had no kind of conversation in Stamford, and so loitered my time away in thus writing a letter now and then, to a distant friend: and in my garden.

Like other intellectuals of his time, such as Isaac Newton, he retained his enthusiasm for investigating curious phenomena. He went on to prove that earthquakes were the result of electrical disturbances of the air of which the movement of the Earth was a secondary effect, that sponges were not living creatures and that the deluge took place in the Autumn. Of all of Stamford's curious people it is probably Stukeley who fully deserves the title of 'Stamford legend', and inspite of his attitude to the town, his work on Stamford has contributed significantly to its rich mythology.

102

APPENDIX
THE
STAMFORD
TAURUS

Ere the sun had painted with gold the village spires, our bullards left their pillows, and, drest for the occasion, assembled in our streets. Looking up to Heaven, as if imploring assistance, one of the bullards imagined he saw somewhat resembling TAURUS, which observation gained him great applause... Another gained equal credit by observing, that he saw something resembling CYGNUS; and in all probability, many other signs would have been discovered in the Zodiac, had not their attention been arrested by the appearance of a real Bull.
Lincoln, Rutland and Stamford Gazette, 15 November, 1796.

Truth, sir, is a cow, which will yield such people no more milk, and so they are gone to milk the bull.
(ed.) **Hill and Powell,** *Boswell's Life of Johnson*, i 444.

HE TWENTIETH century has witnessed a radical new interest in alternative science and archaeology, generated by a new religious philosophy based on the idea of oneness with nature. A New Age in historical interpretation has arrived which is comparable to the pioneering work of the great eighteenth-century antiquarians such as William Stukeley.

In 1922, Alfred Watkins shocked the traditional academic world when he showed in his book, *The Old Straight Track,* that ancient historical sites were aligned along straight lines of mystic energy, commonly known as ley lines. Only three years later Katherine Maltwood, FRSA, discovered one of the most important geomantic sites in the world, the Glastonbury Zodiac, and published her remarkable findings in two seminal works: *Glastonbury's Temple of the Stars, Enchantments of Britain* and *An Aerial Survey*. Since then the study of New Age sciences, such as geomancy, astro-archaeology and divination, has brought about a whole new understanding which totally challenges our conventional preconceptions. Recently Iman Wilkens has proved through an exhaustive study of Homer that Troy stood, not in Turkey, but on the site of a filling station off the A604 south east of Cambridge.

In 1989, historians and archaeologists using these new techniques discovered that Stamford was built on the site of an ancient geomantic earthwork representing a running bull. Geomancy, according to Nigel Pennick, is 'the science of putting human habitats and activities into harmony with the visible and invisible world around us', and such sites become 'cosmic power points on the surface of the earth, special places where the mind can expand into new levels of consciousness, places where visions, transcendental states of prophecy, may be experienced'. This means that ancient man deliberately shaped his environment to make it represent a part of the cosmic whole, an access point into the world of the gods. Such geomantic figures are comparable with Christian cathedrals and were inspired by a similar devotion

Stamford lies at the crossing of several ancient prehistoric trackways, and, as these tracks were often aligned on ley lines, it is likely that the site of Stamford is an energy power point in much the same way as Avebury or Glastonbury is. Instead of a stone circle a Taurean earthwork was created using 'Spiritual Engineering' probably in the period 1800-1600BC. It was formed by altering the topographical aspect of the land immediately north of the River Welland and the running figure of the Bull from east to west across the town is reminiscent of a Cretan bull cult fresco at the Palace of Minos at Knossos of the same period. Indeed, the Stamford Taurus might have been formed by early Mycenean settlers, as a representation of a Mycenean dagger carved into Stonehenge proves that people of that race were in Britain at the time. Troy was only forty miles away to the south east which confirms that this was an important area of early settlement.

But why should Stamford have a bull image? One theory is that the town was once part of a vast cosmic Zodiac which radiated from Stonehenge. The town lies on a direct line from Stonehenge that passes straight through *Oxford*, and this seems to confirm that Stamford was the Taurean astrological figure in this system. The reference to the Zodiac in the *Stamford Gazette* in 1796 certainly supports this theory but many of the other astrological signs have been lost (although Glastonbury has been associated with Aquarius) and the concept is difficult to prove. An alternative explanation is that the figure indicates the existence of an important fertility bull cult at Stamford which was brought over by the Myceneans. G. Higgins in *Celtic Druids* reminds us that 'The remains of the worship of the bull, or the sun in Taurus, are met with everywhere - all over India, Persia, Greece, Italy and Britain.' This would mean that Stamford was not only one of the major religious sites of old Albion, but it was also part of a Taurean bull cult extending over the whole world.

From the creation of the geomantic bull image evolved the unique bull-running festival. The traditional tale of Earl Warrenne founding the custom in 1209 was a later attempt by establishment writers and the Christian Church to play down the early pagan origin of the custom. The early bull-running was administered by a secret guild of mason-like bull priests who were closely associated with the ancient university. It is probable that the university buildings were sited on the line of the geomantic Taurean figure and this pagan connection accounts for the violent suppression of the university by the Pope in the early seventh century.

The geomantic form of the bull is seen today through the deliberate siting of the town's medieval churches and religious houses on the ancient pagan sites that defined the bull's shape. This proves that the geomantic tradition was still very much alive at that time, supported by alchemists and in this case by the bull priests. It also explains various unresolved questions regarding the town's plan and development. It explains why Stamford had so many churches, rather than the more common single church, as at Grantham and Newark. A large number of churches was necessary to form the topographical power points of the astrological figure (there are traditionally twenty points in the

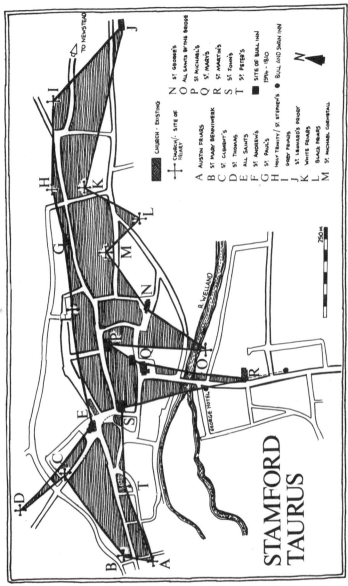

The Stamford Taurus based on original plans and diagrams made by the Brazenose
Society in 1985 using aerial photographic evidence.

BULL LEAPING FROM KNOSSOS FRESCO c. 1800 BC

representation). This resulted in the construction of churches that could not possibly have been supported by such a small population - there were fifteen in the town centre alone - and these were maintained by the bull priests for secret ritual and ceremonial services on 13 November, the 'festal day'. The persecution of the bull cult in the later medieval period combined with the ruthless sack of the town in 1461 forced the closure of many of these smaller churches: St. Mary's Bynwerk, St. Clement's, St. Thomas', St. Andrew's, St. Paul's, St. Stephen's, St. Michael's Cornstall, All Saints' by the Bridge and St. Peter's all disappeared.

The strict constraints upon the siting of the churches also helps to explain their unusual layout. The extraordinary proximity of All Saints and St. John's is explained by the fact that they form the neck of the bull. St. Peter's and the adjacent castle site form part of the bull's head, as these important pagan sites were the first to be rebuilt in the medieval period. St. Thomas's isolated position, well outside the medieval town wall, is explained by the bull's horn and St. Martin's Church forms the front leg of the running bull - the medieval guild of that church being responsible for providing the bull for the bull-running festival.

The rear section of the bull to the east is identified by the medieval monastery sites. The stubby third leg is probably the result of the difficulty of building on the marshy ground near the River Welland, although it has been suggested that the 'Blackfriars Spur' forms the phallus of the bull. The tail of the bull has become a contentious issue amongst geomantic experts. It has been suggested that the

107

thirteenth-century Newstead Priory forms the terminus of the tail, but the Mycenean custom of removing the tail of the sacred bull implies that the Stamford figure may never have had one.

Knowledge of the geomantic alignment of Stamford was deliberately suppressed in the period following the Reformation, when the monastic sites were dissolved. The siting of the Bull Inn on the line of the figure in 1594 shows that the belief persisted and the location of the Bull and Swan in St. Martin's was a conscious eighteenth-century reference to the tradition, being positioned on the line of the front leg. By this time it was only the bullards and the newly created orders of masons that held the knowledge of the bull. The discovery of a masonic mural in the George Hotel in March 1985, right on the line of the geomantic figure, proves that the lodge was positioned according to ancient laws. Later historians working in the usual restricted academic conventions failed to recognise the bull figure and the Christian gentry of the town attempted to suppress the bull-running custom throughout the late eighteenth and early nineteenth centuries. The report in the *Stamford Gazette* on 15 November 1796, quoted at the begining of this article, indicates that the bullards' faith continued despite this opposition. The custom was finally stopped in 1839 and Stamford's Taurean significance was lost.

Stamford must have been one of the religious and academic Meccas of ancient Albion, situated close to Troy, and a place of international pilgrimage for both mystics and scholars. It was the geomantic sign and the powerful bull guild which persuaded Bladud to found the first university in the world at Stamford, and its influence made the town prosperous and important in the Middle Ages. The later ignorance of the bull figure resulted in Stamford's decline into a small provincial town, but the rediscovery of Stamford's Taurean past will hopefully once more bring prosperity and glory to this famous town.

BIBLIOGRAPHY

Andrews, William, *Bygone Lincolnshire*, 2 volumes (Hull, 1891).

The Anglo-Saxon Chronicle, edited by Dorothy Whitelock, David Douglas and Susie Tucker (London, 1961).

Anon., *A True Relation of Colonell Cromwels Proceedings against the Cavaliers Sent in a Letter from a Gentleman in his Army* (London, 1643).

Anon., *The Life of that Wonderful and Extraordinary Heavy Man, the late Daniel Lambert, from his Birth to the moment of his Dissolution, with an account of Men noted for their Corpulency and other interesting matter* (Stamford, 1809).

Anon., *Courtship and Marriage of Henry Cecil* (Peterborough, late 19th century)

Bede, *Bede's Ecclesiastical History of the English People*, ed. B. Colgrave and R. Mynors (Oxford, 1969).

Billing, J. Clare, *Stamford and its Historians* (copy in Stamford Museum, c.1950s).

Blore, Thomas, *An Account of the Public Schools, Hospitals, and other Charitable Foundations in the Borough of Stanford* (Stamford, 1813).

Bolle, Kees W., 'Myth and Mythology', *Encyclopaedia Britannica*, 15th ed. (1974), Macropaedia, XII, pp.793-804.

Brand, John, *Observations on the Popular Antiquities of Great Britain* Vols.1-3, ed. Sir Henry Ellis (London, 1853).

Brewer, E. Cobham, *Dictionary of Phrase and Fable* (London, 1870).

Briggs, Katharine M., *A Dictionary of British Folk-Tales* (Bloomington U.S.A., 1971).

Burton, George, *Chronology of Stamford* (Stamford, 1846).

Burton, G. H., *Rambles Around Stamford* (Stamford, 1872).

Burton, George H., *Old Lincolnshire* (Stamford, 1883-5).
   Bull-running, pp.90-5, 107-15, 129-35, 161-6, 191-2, 227-8.

Burton, G. H., *Guide to Stamford and Neighbourhood* (Stamford, 1896).

Burton, George H., *Stamford Bull-Running, Its Sport, Its History, Its Music, Its Song* (Stamford, 1927).

Bushaway, Bob, *By Rite: Custom, Ceremony and Community in England 1700-1880* (London, 1982).

Butcher, Richard, *The Survey and the Antiquities of the Towne of Stamford* (Stamford, 1646; reprint, 1717).

Camden, William, *Britannia*, ed. Edmund Gibson (London, 1695).

Candidus, Hugh, *The Peterborough Chronicle of Hugh Candidus with La Geste De Burgh*, edited by William Mellows and A. Bell (London, 1949).

Capgrave, John, *Nova Legenda Angliae* (Oxford, 1901).

Clarke, David T. D., *Daniel Lambert*, 2nd edition (Leicester, 1973).

Cross, Colin, *The Fascists of Britain* (London, 1961).

Crowley, Rev. Theodore, 'Roger Bacon', *Encyclopaedia Britannica*, 15th ed. (1974), Macropaedia, II, pp. 567-8.

Dennis, G. Ravenscroft, *The House of Cecil* (London, 1914).

[Drakard, John], *History of Stamford* (Stamford, 1822).

Drayton, Michael, *Poly-Olbion* (first 18 songs published London, 1612; completed volume first published London, 1622).

Dyer, T. F. Thiselton, *British Popular Customs* (London, 1876).

Evans, Bergen, *Dictionary of Mythology* (London, 1970).

Farmer, David Hugh, *Oxford Dictionary of Saints* (Oxford, 1979).

Gardiner, S. R., *History of the Great Civil War, Vol. 3* (London, 1891).

Gilbert, St., *The Book of St. Gilbert*, ed. Raymonde Foreville and Gillian Keir (Oxford, 1987), pp. 112-15.

Gildas, *Gildas' The Ruin of Britain and Other Works*, ed. Michael Winterbottom (London and Chichester, 1978).

Graystanes, Robertus de, *Historia de Statu Ecclesiae Dunelmensis* in [(ed.) Raine, James] *Historia Dunelmensis Scriptores Tres* (London and Edinburgh, 1839), publications of the Surtees Society, Volume 9.

Gutch, Mrs. and Peacock, Mabel, *County Folklore Volume V, Lincolnshire* (London, 1908).

Hackwood, Frederick William, *Staffordshire Customs, Superstitions and Folklore* (Lichfield, 1924).

Hardyng, John, *Chronicle from the Earliest Period of English History Together with the Continuation by Richard Grafton*, ed. Henry Ellis (London, 1812).

[Harrod, William], *The Antiquities of Stamford and St. Martin's* (Stamford, 1785).

Hartley, John S. and Rogers, Alan, *The Religious Foundations of Medieval Stamford* (Nottingham, 1974).

Higden, Ranulph, *Polychronicon Randulphi Higden monachi Cestrensis*, ed. Churchill Babington and J. R. Lumby, 9 vols., Rolls Series (London, 1865-86).

Higgins, John, *The first parte of the Mirour for Magistrates, containing the Falles of the first Infortunate Princes of this Lande* (London, 1575).

[Howgrave, Francis], *An Essay on the Ancient and Present State of Stamford* (Stamford, 1726).

Huntingdon, Henry of, *The Chronicle of Henry of Huntingdon*, trans. Thomas Forester (London, 1853).

Inglis-Jones, Elizabeth, *The Lord of Burghley* (London, 1964).

[Ingulph], *Ingulph's Chronicle of the Abbey of Crowland*, trans. Henry T. Riley (London, 1854), pp.153-5.

Jackson, Margaret, *Chronology of Stamford 1840-1975* (unpublished manuscript in Stamford Museum).

Jewell, Brian, *Fairs and Revels* (Tunbridge Wells, 1976).

Leach, A. F, 'Stamford University' in *Victoria History of the County of Lincoln vol II*, ed. William Page (London, 1906), pp.468-74.

Lecky, W. E. H., *History of the Rise and Influence of the Spirit of Rationalism in Europe*, 3rd edition (London, 1866).

Leland, John, *The Itinerary of John Leland* Vols 1-5, ed. Lucy Toulmin Smith (London,1964).

Lincolnshire Notes and Queries (Horncastle, 1849-1905).

Lovegrove, E. W., 'The Churches of Stamford' in *Stamford and its Surroundings* (London, 1908).

Madan, Falconer, 'The Name and Arms of the College: With Some Account of the Brazen Nose and the Stamford Migration', *Monograph* II (each monograph is separately paginated) in Falconer Madan, E. W. Allfrey and A. J. Butler, *Brasenose College Quatercentenary Monographs* (Oxford, 1909).

Maltwood, K. E., *A Guide to Glastonbury's Temple of the Stars* (Cambridge, 1964; first published 1929).

Monmouth, Geoffrey of, *History of the Kings of Britain*, trans. Sebastian Evans and Charles Dunn (London, 1963).

Murder Casebook No.6, The Acid Bath Murders (London, 1990).

[Nennius], *Nennius' British History and The Welsh Annals*, ed. John Morris (London and Chichester, 1980).

Nevinson, Rev. C., *History of Stamford* (Stamford, 1879).

Newton, David, *Mercury Mystery*, (Stamford, 1988).

Owen, Robert, *The Life of Robert Owen* (1857-8).

Peacock, Mabel, 'Notes on the Stamford Bull-running' in *Folklore* 15 (1904), pp.199-203.

Peck, Francis, *The History of the Stamford Bull-Runnings: Containing the Original and Progress of that Elegant Diversion* (Stamford, n.d., possibly 1723).

Peck, Francis, *Antiquarian Annals of Stanford* (London, 1727, reprinted 1979).

Peck, Francis, *Desiderata Curiosa* (London, 1732, 1735).

Pennick, Ann, 'Underground Tunnels of Glastonbury' in *Glastonbury, Ancient Avalon, New Jerusalem*, ed., Anthony Roberts (London, 1978).

Pennick, Nigel, *The Ancient Science of Geomancy* (London, 1979).

Piggott, Stuart, 'The Druidic Rector of All Saints' in *Stamford Historian* (Nottingham), No.1 1977, pp. 5-7.

Piggott, Stuart, *William Stukeley - An Eighteenth Century Antiquarian*, 2nd edition, (London 1985).

Piper, Alan, 'St. Leonard's Priory, Stamford' in *Stamford Historian* (Nottingham), No.5 1980, pp. 5-25, No.6 1982.

Rivet, A. L. F. and Smith, Colin, *The Place Names of Roman Britain* (London, 1979).

Rogers, Alan, editor, *The Making of Stamford* (Leicester, 1965).

Rogers, Alan, Stamford Survey Group, *The Medieval Buildings of Stamford* (Nottingham 1970).

Rogers, Alan, *The Book of Stamford* (Buckingham, 1983).

Royal Commission on the Historical Monuments of England, *The Town of Stamford* (London, 1977).

Salter, H. E., 'The Stamford Schism', from *The English Historical Review*, 37 (1922), pp.249-53.

Sandall, T., *Reminiscences of Old Stamford - An Account of the Last Bull-Runnings* (Pamphlet of article taken from *Stamford and Rutland Guardian*, 4 December 1915).

Sayce, Archibald Henry, 'The Legend of King Bladud' in *Y Cymmroder* 10 (1889), pp.207-21.

Scott, J. M., *Boadicea* (London, 1975).

Seymour, William, *Battles in Britain, Vol. 1, 1066-1547* (London, 1975).

Sharp, Samuel, *History and Descriptive Sketch of Stamford* (Stamford, 1847).

Simpson, Justin, 'Stamford Waits and their Predecessors', from *The Reliquary* (July 1885).

Smith, George, *Dictionary of National Biography* (Oxford, 1948).

Stamford and Rutland Guardian, from archive at *Stamford Mercury* office.

Stamford Historical Society, Stamford Survey Group, *Stamford Historian* (Nottingham, 1978-1980).

Stamford Mercury, from archive at *Stamford Mercury* office, Sheepmarket, Stamford.

Stukeley, William, *Designs of Stamford Antiquities* (unpublished, 1735).

Stukeley, William, *The Family Memoirs of the Rev. William Stukeley, M. D.*, published by Surtees Society (London, 3 vols., 1882, 1883, 1887).

Stukeley, William, *Diaries*, 2 volumes, unpublished. Edited extracts by Michael Key in *Stamford Historian*, No. 3, February 1979, pp. 22-8, No. 4, February 1980, pp. 42-5.

Tennyson, Alfred, *Poems* (1842).

Tickell, Rev. S. Claude, *Guide to Old Stamford* (Stamford, 1906).

Till, Eric C., *A Family Affair, Stamford and the Cecils 1650-1900* (Rugby, 1990)

Town Guide books of the twentieth century, collection in Stamford Museum.

Walcott, MacKenzie, E. C., *Memorials of Stamford* (Stamford, 1867, reprint, 1902).

Walker, Henry, *Stamford with its Surroundings* (London, 1908).

Waterfield, A. J., *Annals of Stamford* (Stamford, 1887).

Watson, S. J., *The Cottage Countess - An Historical Romance* (Dublin, 1974).

Westminster, Matthew of, *Flores Historiarum* Vol II, ed. C. D. Yonge (London, 1853).

Wilkens, Iman J., *Where Troy Once Stood* (London, 1990).

Winks, J. F., *The Bull-Running at Stamford, a Sermon* (London, 1829).

Wood, E. Bentley, *Legends of Stamford* (Stamford, n.d., c.1888).

Wood, E. Bentley, *ed.*, 'The Tragedie of Bladud the Legendary Founder of the University of Stamford' reprinted from Higgin's *The Mirour for Magistrates of 1575* (Stamford, 1889).

Wood, E. Bentley, *1461 - An Epoch in the History of Stamford* (Stamford, 1889).

Wood, E. Bentley, personal books of press cuttings relating to local historical matters, 4 volumes, Phillips Collection, Stamford Town Hall.

Wood, E. G. de Salis, *The University of Stamford* (Peterborough, 1932).